PRAISE FOR *BUILDING A STORYBRAND*

"This is a seminal book built around an idea that will clarify, energize, and transform your business. Donald Miller offers a specific, detailed, and useful way to change the way you talk about the work you care about."

—Seth Godin, author of *All Marketers Are Liars*

"StoryBrand is the best thing to happen to my conversions in a long time. After rewriting one webinar registration page using the StoryBrand framework, the page converted at 60 percent to a cold ads audience. That's UNHEARD of! I especially love that StoryBrand always puts the customer first, which aligns with my company's core values. (And it doesn't hurt that sales have never been better!) We now use the StoryBrand framework for every sales page . . . home page . . . email . . . anywhere in my business that we write copy."

—Amy Porterfield, *New York Times* bestselling author of *Two Weeks Notice* and Host of *Online Marketing Made Easy* podcast

"Donald Miller ought to be working with your company just like he worked with ours. We changed our website after learning his framework and the results were fantastic. We noticed a difference right away. The StoryBrand framework works—and we are implementing it companywide. Read this book!"

—Ken Blanchard, chief spiritual officer of The Ken Blanchard Companies and coauthor of *The New One Minute Manager®*

"Donald Miller will teach you a lot more than how to sell products; he will teach you how to transform the lives of your customers. Your customers need you to play a role in their lives, and this book will teach you how. If you want your business to grow, read this book."

—John C. Maxwell, #1 *New York Times* bestselling author

"This is the most important business/marketing book of the year. All communicators know the power of story. Donald Miller has captured the process to make your marketing pierce the white noise of the most overserved marketing generation in history. You *have* to read this book!"

—Dave Ramsey, #1 *New York Times* bestselling author

"Donald Miller reminds us that all good messaging begins and ends with empathy. He knows that if you want to be seen, heard, and understood, the first step is to listen. Get this book if you want to connect with people in a profound way."

—Bill Haslam, forty-ninth governor of Tennessee

"If you like making money, read this book. The StoryBrand framework will help you create sales messages that people listen and respond to. We use it all the time, and it works!"

—Ryan Deiss, founder and CEO of DigitalMarketer

"*Building a StoryBrand* isn't just about clarifying your message, it's about clarifying your mission. Playing the role of Guide so you can help Heroes win in their own story must be a foundational drive if we expect to transform our customers' lives. In this book, Don Miller shows us all how to find incredible meaning in our work by doing exactly that."

—Will Guidara, Author of *Unreasonable Hospitality*

"I've been using Don Miller's StoryBrand framework in my business for years now. It's the single best marketing tool I know. We use it on every product we launch. I've had Don personally teach my company and clients, and I recommend him to everyone. Now, all these revolutionary insights are easily accessible between these covers."

—Michael Hyatt, *New York Times* bestselling author and Founder, Full Focus

"*Building a StoryBrand* is your guide to cutting through the noise and making your message resonate. Donald Miller's wisdom shows us how to draw customers into a story where they're the heroes of their own transformation. This isn't just a book—it's an inspiring journey that'll ignite your passion and elevate your impact!"

– Jenna Kutcher, Host of *The Goal Digger Podcast* and *New York Times* Bestselling Author of *How Are You, Really?*

BUILDING A STORYBRAND 2.0

Clarify Your Message So Customers Will Listen

DONALD MILLER

HarperCollins Leadership
An Imprint of HarperCollins

Building a StoryBrand 2.0

Published by HarperCollins Leadership, an imprint of HarperCollins Publishers.

The author is represented by Ambassador Literary Agency, Nashville, TN.

Graphics designed by Kyle Reid.

ISBN 978-1-4002-4887-2 (HC)
ISBN 978-1-4002-4888-9 (eBook)
ISBN 978-1-4002-5130-8 (IE)

Library of Congress Control Number: 2017937432

Printed in the United States of America

24 25 26 27 28 LBC 5 4 3 2 1

This book is dedicated to:
The team at Coach Builder, Business Made Simple, and StoryBrand. It's been the greatest pleasure of my career to build a business with you.
You are living proof that when friends sacrifice together for a common good, they can become family.

CONTENTS

WANT YOUR ENTIRE TEAM TO UNDERSTAND THE STORYBRAND FRAMEWORK?

We noticed many business leaders wanted their teams to better understand the StoryBrand framework and were looking for a tool to easily explain it to them. To help, we created a 1920s-style radio theater production that teaches the framework by telling a story. The story is about two brothers challenged with saving their mother's board game company. Can the brothers save the company? How does StoryBrand help them? Will the brothers' friendship survive the challenge? You can find out by listening to *StoryBrand Radio Theater Presents: Pete and Joe Save Their Mother's Company*, available now, on Audible or Youtube.com/@storybrand.

NOTE FROM THE AUTHOR ON THIS UPDATED EDITION

Since its initial publication in 2017, *Building a StoryBrand* has sold more than one million copies. The book has now helped small and large businesses alike create sound bites they can repeat to grow their businesses, and the results have been better than good. I would safely estimate this book has helped companies realize billions in increased revenue and millions of new customers. The framework has been utilized to sell everything from plungers to American foreign policy to airplane engines.

In this updated edition, I hope I have made the book even more helpful. To do this, I've nearly doubled the examples and stories of how brands have used the framework to endear and engage customers. Nearly a million businesses have used the free online BrandScript tool that comes with this book, and we've worked hard to improve the process and results.

For the rerelease of *Building a StoryBrand*, we've taken the cumulative content I've personally developed—including all my teachings, books, YouTube videos, podcasts, and recorded coaching sessions—to inform our own StoryBrand Brain that will create a custom StoryBrand Messaging and Marketing Campaign for your brand or product.

We believe we've created the greatest artificial intelligence tool for messaging and marketing on the internet. After you respond to our prompts and answer about five minutes' worth of questions, the StoryBrand Brain will generate a robust report, including a tagline, one-liner, wireframed website, lead generator, follow-up emails, sales script, narrative scripts for YouTube videos and social media, podcast prompts and topics, bonus ideas to create urgency, upsell product ideas, plug-and-play social media posts, plus industry trends specific to your industry.

This new edition of *Building a StoryBrand* will be helpful whether you are starting a brand, growing an existing brand, positioning yourself as a leader, are a sales rep for an existing company, or even growing a nonprofit. The book will help you do these things by helping you discover the words you can use on websites, marketing and messaging campaigns, keynote presentations, proposals, sales letters, sales conversations, and even sound bites you can repeat in casual conversation.

Ultimately, your brand will grow faster when you use the right words. I wrote (and rewrote) this book to help you find those words.

To create your StoryBrand Messaging and Marketing Campaign, go to StoryBrand.AI.

I also hope this new version of the book is fun to read. After you've created your sound bites, my hope is that many people will enjoy the story you invite them into.

INTRODUCTION

This is not a book about telling your company's story. A book like that would be a waste of time. Customers generally don't care about your story; they care about their own.

Your customer should be the hero of the story, not your brand. This is the secret every phenomenally successful business understands.

What follows is a seven-part framework that will change the way you talk about your business and perhaps the way you *do* business.

Each year we help more than ten thousand businesses stop wasting money on marketing and grow their company by helping them clarify their message. This framework will work for you, regardless of your industry.

To get the most out of this book, I encourage you to do three things:

1. Read the book and understand the SB7 framework.
2. Filter your message through the framework to create a StoryBrand Messaging and Marketing Campaign.
3. Execute your new marketing and messaging strategy to see results.

Marketing has changed. Businesses that invite their customers into a heroic story will grow. Businesses that don't will be forgotten.

May we all be richly rewarded for putting our customers' stories above our own.

SECTION 1

WHY MOST MARKETING IS A MONEY PIT

CHAPTER 1

THE KEY TO BEING SEEN, HEARD, AND UNDERSTOOD

Most companies waste enormous amounts of money on marketing. We all know how mind-numbing it is to spend precious dollars on a new marketing effort that gets no results. When we see the reports, we wonder what went wrong or, worse, whether our product is really as good as we thought it was.

But what if the problem wasn't the product? What if the problem was the way we talked about the product?

The problem is simple: the graphic artists and designers we're hiring to build our websites and ad campaigns have degrees in design and know everything about Photoshop, but they haven't read a single book about writing good sales copy. How many of them know how to clarify your message so customers listen? Even worse, these companies will gladly take your money regardless of whether you see positive results.

The fact is, pretty websites don't sell things. Words sell things. And if we haven't clarified our message, our customers won't listen.

If we pay a lot of money to a design agency without first clarifying our message, we might as well be holding a bullhorn up to a monkey. The only thing a potential customer will hear is noise.

Still, clarifying our message isn't easy. I had one client say that when he tried to do so, he felt like he was inside the bottle trying to read the label. I understand. Before I started StoryBrand I was a writer and spent thousands of hours staring at a blank computer screen, wondering what to say. That soul-wrenching frustration led me to create a communication framework based on the proven power of story, and I swear it was like discovering a secret formula. Using the framework, my writing got easier and better. I ended up selling millions of books. After using the framework to create clear messages in my books, I used it to filter the marketing collateral in my own small company. Once we got clear, we doubled in revenue for four consecutive years. I now teach that framework to more than ten thousand businesses each year.

Once they get their message straight, our clients create quality websites, incredible keynote presentations, emails that get opened, advertising that gets clicked, social media posts that get noticed, and sales letters that people respond to. Why? Because nobody will listen to you if your message isn't clear, no matter how expensive your marketing collateral may be.

At StoryBrand we've had clients double, triple, and even quadruple their revenue after they got one thing straight—their message.

The StoryBrand framework has been just as effective for

billion-dollar brands as it has for mom-and-pop businesses. It is just as powerful for American corporations as it has been for those in Japan and Africa. Why? Because the human brain, no matter what region of the world it comes from, is drawn toward clarity and away from confusion.

The reality is we aren't just in a race to get our products to market; we're also in a race to communicate why our customers need those products. Even if we have the best product in the marketplace, we'll lose to an inferior product if our competitor's offer is communicated more clearly.

So what's your message? Can you say it easily? Is it simple, relevant, and relatable? Can your entire team repeat your company's message in such a way that it is compelling? Can you and your team easily remember the talking points they can use to describe what the company offers and why every potential customer should buy it?

How many sales are we missing out on because customers can't figure out what our offer is within five seconds of visiting our website, seeing our ads, reading our lead generators, or opening our emails?

WHY SO MANY BUSINESSES FAIL

To find out why so many marketing and branding attempts fail, I called my friend Mike McHargue. Mike, often called "Science Mike" because he hosts a successful podcast called *Ask Science Mike*, spent fifteen years using science-based methodologies to help companies figure out how their customers think, specifically in the tech space. Sadly, he left advertising when a client asked him to create an algorithm predicting the associated buying habits of people with diabetes. Translation: they wanted him to sell junk food to diabetics. Mike refused and left the industry. He's a good man. I called, though, because he still has incredible insight as to how marketing, story, and behavior all blend together.

At my request, Mike flew to Nashville to attend one of our workshops. After two days learning the StoryBrand 7-Part framework (hereafter called the SB7 framework), we sat on my back porch and I grilled him with questions. Why does this formula work? What's happening in the brains of consumers as they encounter a message filtered through this formula? What's the science behind why brands like Apple and Coke, who intuitively use this formula, dominate the marketplace?

"There's a reason most marketing collateral doesn't work," Mike said, putting his feet up on the coffee table. "Their marketing is too complicated. The brain has to work too hard to process the information. The more simple and predictable the communication, the easier it is for the brain to digest. Story helps because it is a sense-making mechanism. Essentially, story formulas put everything in order so the brain doesn't have to work to understand what's going on."

Mike went on to explain that, among the million things the brain is good at, the overriding function of the brain is to help an individual survive and thrive. Everything the human brain does, all day, involves helping that person (and the people that person cares about) get ahead in life.

Mike asked if I remembered that old pyramid we learned about in high school, Abraham Maslow's hierarchy of needs. First, he reminded me, the brain is tasked with setting up a system in which we can eat and drink and survive physically. In our modern, first-world economy, this means having a job and a dependable income. Then the brain is concerned with safety, which might entail having a roof over our heads and a sense of well-being and power that keeps us from being vulnerable. After food and shelter are taken care of, our brains start thinking about our relationships, which entail everything from reproducing in a sexual relationship, to being nurtured in a romantic relationship, to creating friendships (a tribe) who will stick by us in case of any social threats. Finally, the brain begins to concern itself with greater psychological, physiological, or even spiritual needs that give us a sense of meaning.

What Mike helped me understand is that, without us knowing it, human beings are constantly scanning their environment (even advertising) for information that is going to help them meet their primitive need to *survive*. This means that when we ramble on and on about how we have the biggest manufacturing plant on the West Coast, our customers don't care. Why? Because that information isn't helping them eat, drink, find a mate, fall in love, build a tribe, experience a deeper sense of meaning, or stockpile weapons in case barbarians start coming over the hill behind their cul-de-sac.

So what do customers do when we blast a bunch of noise at them? They ignore us.

And so right there on my back porch, Mike defined two critical mistakes brands make when they talk about their products and services.

Mistake Number One

The first mistake brands make is failing to focus on the aspects of their offer that will help people survive and thrive.

All great stories are about survival—either physical, emotional, relational, or spiritual. A story about anything else won't captivate an audience. Nobody's interested. This means that if we position our products and services as anything but an aid in helping people survive, thrive, be accepted, find love, achieve an aspirational identity, or bond with a tribe that will defend them physically and socially, good luck selling anything to anybody. Surviving and thriving are the primary concerns of every healthy human being on the planet. We can take that truth to the bank. Or to bankruptcy court, should we choose to ignore it as an undeniable fact.

Mike said our brains are constantly sorting through information, so we discard millions of unnecessary facts every day. If we were to spend an hour in a giant ballroom, our brains would never think to count how many chairs are in the room. Meanwhile, we would always know where the exits are. Why? Because our brains don't need to know how many chairs there are in the room to survive, but knowing where the exits are would be helpful in case of a fire.

Mike helped me understand that, without knowing it, the subconscious is always categorizing and organizing information, and, as it relates to growing our businesses, when we talk publicly about our company's random backstory or internal goals, or worse, when we are vague and confusing about what problem we solve for the customer, we're positioning ourselves as the chairs, not the exits. In other words, the way most of us talk about our brand and our products causes the very customers we want to engage us to ignore us.

"The reason many businesses—and for that matter, leaders, are ignored," Mike continued, "is because processing information demands that the brain burn calories. And the burning of too many calories processing information we do not need in order to survive acts against the brain's primary job: to help us survive and thrive."

The point is this: most of our messaging collateral is elusive, confusing, or unrelatable, which means that God has literally designed our customers' brains to ignore us.

Mistake Number Two

The second mistake brands make when they talk about their products and services is they require their customers to burn too many calories in order to understand their offer.

When having to process too much seemingly unnecessary information, people begin to ignore the source of that information in an effort to conserve calories. In other words, there's a survival mechanism within our customers' brains that is designed to tune us out should we ever start confusing them.

Imagine every time we talk about our products to potential customers, they have to start running on a treadmill. Literally, they have to jog the whole time we're talking. How long do you think they're going to pay attention? Not long. And yet this is very close to what's actually happening in our customers' minds as we talk to them about our products. When we start our elevator pitch or keynote address, or when somebody visits our website, they're burning calories to process the information we're sharing. And if we don't say something (and say something quickly) they can use to survive or thrive, they will tune us out.

These two realities—that people are looking for brands that can help them survive and thrive, and that communication must be so simple that a person doesn't have to burn too many mental calories to understand what we're saying—explain why the SB7 framework has helped so many businesses grow their revenue and influence. The key is to create a message that reveals how we help our customers survive and to do so in language so simple that they understand the message without having to, burn too many calories.

Not long ago, I helped a major pet-supply brand nearly double their revenue by adding only three words to their packaging and signage: kids love aquariums. Spectrum brands had been wildly successful in the home aquarium and fish supply market at American pet stores for years; however, they were having trouble selling aquariums to anybody other than fish enthusiasts and hobbyists. Despite their efforts, they were not able to move into the family market. As we spoke, I recalled that my young daughter loved aquariums. In fact, on a recent trip to London she asked me to stand in front of the aquarium in the lobby for long periods of time until we could find Nemo! She loved the aquarium so much I actually took a video of it with my phone so she could watch the video before we read bed-time stories. When I recommended that Spectrum simply add three words to their packaging, *Kids Love Aquariums*, they weren't convinced the answer could be that easy. But think about it: if parents are walking into a pet store looking for something their kids will love (part of the human survival dynamic involves building a family tribe, creating family bonds, and passing love and nurture to our children), then the "Kids Love Aquariums" tagline would position their products as the very solution parents are looking for.

The result of the three-word campaign in a test market? A 99 percent increase in overall sales. The results were so good that Spectrum is currently rolling out the messaging strategy nationwide.

The truth is, you don't need an expensive ad campaign or a beautiful style guide to grow your business; you just need a few sound bites customers immediately understand so they quickly realize you have a solution to their problem.

But what kind of sound bites should we use, and how do we come up with them?

STORY TO THE RESCUE

Story is the most powerful tool we can use to organize and communicate our offering so people don't have to burn many calories to understand us. I discovered this during my years as a memoirist. My first book, which I wrote before understanding story and story structure, sold only about ten thousand copies. But after studying and incorporating a story-based formula, my next book ended up on the *New York Times* bestseller list for nearly a year. Story, it turns out, is a sense-making device readers can follow without having to burn very many calories.

What is a story? A story identifies an ambition or objective the hero wants to accomplish, then defines the challenges that are keeping the hero from getting what they want, then provides a plan to help the hero conquer those challenges so they can survive and thrive. It's an age-old formula, but it works. And it doesn't only work to entertain us; it works to get our attention. Here, then, is the thesis of this book: when we define the elements of a story as it relates to our brand, we create a mental map customers can follow to engage our products and services.

In the years since the first edition of this book came out, hundreds of thousands of business owners have used the framework to invite their customers into a story, and the results are compelling. Thousands of business owners and leaders have told us that, after simply clarifying their message, sales have grown exponentially.

Still, when I talk about story to business leaders, they immediately put me in a category with artists, thinking I want to introduce them to something fanciful. But that's not what I'm talking about. I'm talking about a concrete formula we can use to garner attention from otherwise distracted customers. I'm talking about practical steps we can take to make sure people see us, hear us, and understand exactly why they simply *must* engage our products.

THE FORMULA FOR CLEAR COMMUNICATION

Formulas are simply the summation of best practices, and the reason we like them is because they work. We've been given great formulas for management, like Ken Blanchard's Situational Leadership, and ones we can use in manufacturing like Six Sigma and Lean Manufacturing. But what about one for communication? Why don't we have a formula we can use to effectively explain what our products offer the world?

The StoryBrand framework is that formula. We know it works because some variation of this formula has been actively used over thousands of years to get people to pay attention to plays, books, and more recently movies and television shows. Talk about a summation of best practices. Story formulas have been tested by the entertainment industry since antiquity. When it comes to grabbing people's attention, this proven formula will be your most powerful ally.

I will warn you though. Story formulas are just that—they are formulaic. Once you know the formulas screenwriters and novelists use to hook a reader, you can predict the path most stories will take. I've learned these formulas so well that my wife hates going to movies with me because she knows at some point I'm going to elbow her and whisper something like, "That guy's going to die in thirty-one minutes."

Story formulas reveal a well-worn path in the human brain, and if we want to stay in business, we need to position our products along a path they are designed to follow.

The good news is these formulas can work just as well at growing your business as they do at entertaining an audience.

THE KEY IS CLARITY

The narrative coming out of a company (and, for that matter, being spoken inside a company) must be clear. In a story, audiences must always know who the hero is, what the hero wants, who the hero has to defeat to get what they want, what tragic thing will happen if they don't win, and what wonderful thing will happen if they do. If an audience can't answer these basic questions, they'll check out and the movie will lose millions at the box office. And if a screenwriter breaks these rules, they'll likely never work again.

The same is true for the brand you represent. Our customers have burning questions, and if we aren't answering those questions, they'll move on to another brand. For example, if we haven't identified what our customer wants, what problem we are helping them solve, and what life will look like after they engage our products and services, we can forget about thriving in the marketplace. Most businesses fail to create these sound bites, and worse, won't stop using confusing or unrelatable language. Whether we're writing a story or attempting to sell products, our message must be clear. Always.

In fact, at StoryBrand we have a mantra: "If you confuse, you'll lose."

BUSINESS HAS AN ENEMY

Clarity is important because your business has a fierce, insidious enemy that, if not identified and combated, will contort what you offer the world into an unrecognizable mess. The enemy I'm talking about is noise.

Noise has killed more ideas, products, and services than taxes, recessions, lawsuits, climbing interest rates, and even inferior product design. I'm not talking about the noise inside our business; I'm talking about the noise we *create* as a business. What we often call marketing is really just clutter and confusion sprayed all over our websites, emails, and commercials. And it's costing us millions.

Years ago, a StoryBrand client who attended one of our workshops pushed back. "I don't think this will work for me," he said. "My business is too diverse to reduce down to a series of sound bites." I asked him to explain.

"I have an industrial painting company with three different revenue streams. In one division we powder coat auto parts. In another we apply sealant to concrete, and in another we have a sterilized painting process used specifically in hospitals."

His business was diverse, but nothing so complex that it couldn't be simplified so more people would hire him. I asked if I could put his website on the giant television screen so the entire workshop could see it. His website was thoughtful, but it didn't make a great deal of sense from an outside perspective (which is how every customer views your business).

The man had hired a fine arts painter to create a painting of his building (was he selling a building?), and at first glance it looked like the website for an Italian restaurant. The first question I had when I went to the website was, "Do you serve free breadsticks?" There were a thousand links ranging from contact information to FAQs to a timeline of the company's history. There were even links to the nonprofits the business supported. It was as though he was using his website to answer a hundred questions, none of which his customers were asking.

I asked the class to raise their hands if they thought my new friend's business would grow if he wiped the website clean and simply featured an image of a guy in a white lab coat painting something next to text that read, "We Paint All Kinds of S#*%," accompanied by a button in the middle of the page that said, "Get a Quote."

The entire class raised their hands in agreement that the new, simple message would increase customer engagement.

Of course his business would grow with a more simple message. Why? Because he would have finally stopped forcing clients to burn calories thinking about his nonprofit work and his story and his job opportunities and instead offered the one thing that would solve his customers' problems: a good painter.

What we think we are saying to our customers and what our customers actually hear are two different things. And customers make buying decisions based not on what we say but on what they hear.

STOP SAYING THAT

All experienced writers know the key to great writing isn't in what they say; it's in what they don't say. For professional writers there is a general rule: the more we cut out, the better the screenplay or book. Great communicators know the power of keeping it simple—that is, if they want people to pay attention and remember anything they say. But clarifying our message isn't easy. The mathematician and philosopher Blaise Pascal is often credited with sending a long letter stating he simply didn't have time to send a short one.

If we want to connect with customers, we have to stop blasting them with noise.

The beautiful thing about clarifying your message using the SB7 framework is it makes communicating easy. No longer will you sit in front of a blank page wondering what to say on your website, in your elevator pitch, in your email blast, in your Facebook ads, or even in your radio or television commercials.

CLARIFY YOUR MESSAGE

Whether we run a small company or a multibillion-dollar brand, confusing our customers is costing us money. How many of our team members can't explain how we help our customers survive and thrive? How many people are buying from our competition because our competitors have communicated more clearly than we have? How long will we last if we keep talking about aspects of our products our customers don't care about?

Things can be different.

To clarify our message we're going to need a serious formula. This formula needs to organize our thinking, reduce our marketing effort, obliterate confusion, terrify the competition, and then get our businesses growing again. Let's learn about that formula now.

CHAPTER 2

THE SECRET WEAPON THAT WILL GROW YOUR BUSINESS

To help you grow your company, I'm going to guide you in simplifying your message into sound bites that come from seven categories. Once you have these seven messages down, any anxiety you experience while talking about your brand will subside, and customers will be more attracted to what you offer. These sound bites will help you better understand your customers' story and place yourself and your products right smack in the middle of it.

Story, after all, is atomic. Stories have always moved through people to motivate and inspire their actions. Story is the energy that has fueled every human movement and is the one thing that can hold a person's attention for hours as entertainment and for years when it informs a life purpose.

Nobody can look away from a good story. In fact, neuroscientists claim the average human being spends more than

30 percent of their time daydreaming—*unless* they're reading, listening to, or watching a story unfold. Why? Because when we are engaged in a story, the story does the daydreaming for us.

Story is the greatest weapon you have to combat noise because it organizes information in such a way that people are compelled to listen. If you want to bring attention to your brand, you must understand how story works and how to invite customers into a narrative that is compelling.

STORY MAKES MUSIC OUT OF NOISE

Living in Nashville, I've learned quite a bit about the difference between music and noise. Nearly half the friends my wife and I share are musicians. The talent around here is immense. Hardly a dinner party goes by without somebody picking up a guitar.

I could summarize what I've learned about the difference between music and noise by saying my friends make music and I make noise, but there's actually some compelling science involved.

Technically speaking, music and noise are similar. Both are created by traveling sound waves that rattle our eardrums. Music, however, is noise that submits to certain rules that allow the brain to engage on a different level. If I played you a recording of a dump truck backing up, birds chirping, and children laughing, you'd not remember those sounds the next day. But if I played you a Beatles song, you'd likely hum it to yourself for a week.

There is an obvious difference between a well-choreographed piece of music and the sound of a cat chasing a rat through a wind chime factory, which is the equivalent of the average small business website, leader's keynote speech, or sales rep's elevator pitch. The brain remembers music and forgets about noise just like the brain remembers some brands and forgets about others.

Story is similar to music. A good story takes a series of random events and truths and distills them into the essence of what really matters. There's a reason the final cut of a movie is called a final cut. Prior to the theatrical release, a film has gone through rounds upon rounds of edits, dialogue omissions, revisions, and scene deletions. Sometimes entire characters end up on the cutting-room floor. Why? Because storytellers utilize frameworks and filters to cut out the noise. If a character or scene doesn't serve the plot, it has to go.

When clients want to add a bunch of confusion to their marketing message, I ask them to consider the ramifications of doing so if they were writing a screenplay. I mean, what if *The Bourne Identity* were a movie about a spy named Jason Bourne searching for his true identity, but it also included scenes of Bourne trying to lose weight, marry a girl, pass the bar exam, win on *Jeopardy*, and adopt a cat? The audience would likely lose interest. When storytellers bombard people with random information, the audience is forced to burn too many calories to make sense of the drama. As a result, they daydream and walk out of the theater, or in the case of our marketing message, leave us for a competing brand where they place their order.

Why do so many brands create noise rather than music? It's because they don't realize they are creating noise. They actually think people are interested in the random information they're doling out.

This is why we need a filter. The essence of branding is to

create simple, relevant messages we can repeat over and over so that we "brand" ourselves into the public consciousness.

STEVE JOBS AND THE MESSAGE OF APPLE

Apple began to grow into the company they are today only after Steve Jobs began filtering his message through the frameworks that storytellers use to build compelling narratives. His thinking transformed after working with (and partially creating) the genius storytelling factory that is Pixar. When Jobs came back to Apple after being surrounded by professional storytellers, he realized story was the foundation on which every memorable brand had been built.

Just think about the incredible transformation that took place in Steve's life after Pixar. In 1983, Apple launched a computer called Lisa, the last project Jobs worked on before he was let go. Jobs released Lisa with a nine-page ad in the *New York Times* spelling out the computer's technical features. It was nine pages of geek talk nobody outside NASA was interested in. The computer bombed.

When Jobs returned to the company after running Pixar, Apple became customer-centric, simple in their product offering, compelling, and clear in their communication. The first campaign Jobs released after returning from his time at Pixar, then, went from nine pages in the *New York Times* to just two words on billboards all over America: *Think Different.*

When Apple began filtering their communication to make it simple and relevant, they actually stopped featuring computers in most of their advertising. After all, nobody at the time knew why they would need a computer. Instead, they understood their customers were all living, breathing protagonists in stories they felt were uninteresting. Jobs invited those heroes into a better story, one in which they could be different, productive, artistic, and recognized. The offer was clear: if you want to be different, choose Apple. The story they invited the public into involved (1) identifying what their customers wanted (to be seen and heard), (2) defining their customers' challenge (that others didn't recognize their hidden genius), and (3) offering their customers a tool they could use to express themselves (computers and smartphones). Each of these plot points is a pillar in ancient storytelling formulas and is critical for connecting with the public.

I'll teach you about these three pillars and more in the coming chapters, but for now realize the time Apple spent clarifying the role they play in their customers' story is one of the primary factors responsible for their growth.

Notice, though, the story of Apple isn't about Apple; it's about you. You're the hero in the story, and they play a role more like Q in the James Bond franchise: they are the guy you go see when you need a tool to help you win the day.

Despite what acolytes of the cult of Mac may say, whether Apple has the best technology is debatable. "Best" is subjective, of course. But it doesn't matter. People don't buy the best products; they buy the products they can understand and apply to their lives the fastest. Apple has inserted themselves into their customers' story like no other technology company, and as a result, they're not only the largest technology company but one of the top ten largest companies period.[1] If we want our own businesses to grow, we should borrow a page from their playbook. We should clarify our message.

STORY CAN GROW YOUR BUSINESS

To better understand what Steve Jobs learned during his years at Pixar, let's take off our business hats for a few pages and pretend we're learning about story for the first time. Once you understand how story integrates with your brand message, you'll be able to create messaging material (and even a brand strategy) that engages more customers and grows your business. And once you really understand and can apply the framework intuitively, people around the office will wonder how in the world you became such a messaging and marketing genius.

After studying hundreds of movies, novels, plays, and musicals across nearly every imaginable genre, and after having written twelve books of my own along with cowriting a nationally released major motion picture based on one of my books, I've narrowed down the necessary elements of a compelling story to seven basic plot points. If we were writing a full screenplay, of course, we'd need more than this, but for the purposes of understanding and entering into our customers' story, there are only seven critical plot points we need to understand.

Story in a Nutshell

Here is nearly every story you watch, read, or hear in a nutshell: A *character* who wants something encounters a *problem* before they can get it. At the peak of their despair, a *guide* steps into their lives, gives them a *plan*, and *calls them to action*. That action helps them avoid *failure* and experience a *success*.

That's really it. You'll see some form of this structure in every movie you watch, every novel you read, and every story you hear from this moment forward. By understanding the formula I just told you, you can essentially predict what is going to happen in almost every story you encounter. These seven basic plot points are powerful because they work to hold a human being's attention. That's why that formula has been used in countless stories for thousands of years. However, this formula is not stale or tiresome. In fact, these plot points are like chords of music in the sense that you can use them to create an infinite variety of narrative expression. Just like playing the guitar, with these seven chords you can create an infinite number of creative and engaging songs. Varying too far from set chords, however, means a composer risks descending into incomprehensible noise. Music, is, after all, noise submitted to rules. If a songwriter breaks the rules, the audience fails to engage. This idea is just as true for stories as it is for music. If a storyteller fails to identify what the hero wants, or does not include enough conflict, or fails to identify the stakes at play, then they are breaking the "rules of story" and the consequences are dire: the audience stops paying attention and the movie fails at the box office (or more likely never gets approved for production).

What does any of this have to do with growing your business? Everything. The same rules that get and keep a movie audience's attention can also get and keep a customer's attention. And attention is what you need more than anything else. But we will talk more about how to apply story to your business later.

For now, let's look at how this simple story framework plays out in a couple of familiar stories. Once you can recognize the framework in stories, you'll start to understand exactly where the story of your brand is confusing customers and costing you influence.

In the first *Hunger Games* movie, Katniss Everdeen must

compete in a twisted fight-to-the-death tournament forced on the people of Panem by an evil, tyrannical government called the Capitol. The problem she faces is obvious: she must kill or be killed (stakes). Katniss is overwhelmed, underprepared, and outnumbered (a hero in a hole).

Along comes Haymitch, the brash, liquor-loving, grizzled winner of a previous Hunger Games tournament (the Guide). Haymitch assumes the role of Katniss's mentor, helping her hatch a plan to win over the public (a plan). The plan is to get Katniss more sponsors, thereby equipping her with more resources for the fight and increasing her chances of winning.

Here is the first *Hunger Games* story laid out on the StoryBrand grid:

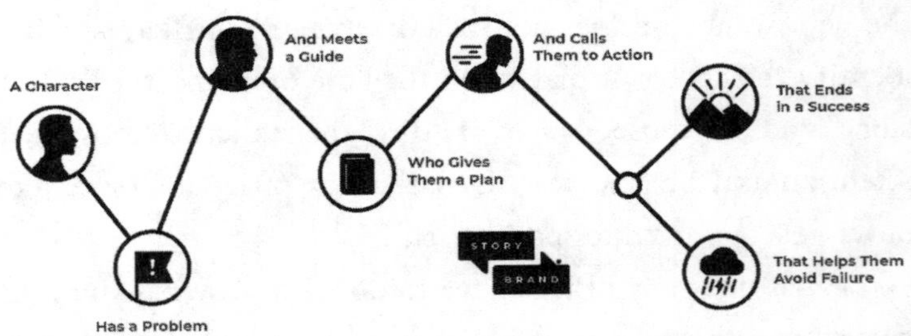

In *Star Wars: A New Hope*, our reluctant hero, Luke Skywalker, experiences a devastating tragedy: His aunt and uncle are murdered at the hands of the evil Empire (a hero in a hole). This sets a series of events in motion: Luke begins the journey of becoming a Jedi Knight (enter a guide, Obi-Wan Kenobi, a former Jedi Knight who once trained Luke's father) and destroys the Empire's battle station, the Death Star, which allows the Rebellion to live and fight another day (the plan).

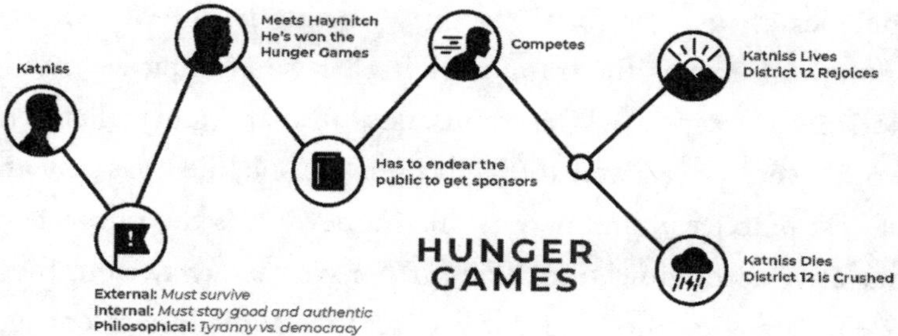

Not every story works this way, but most do. Sometimes a writer will bring in multiple guides or (usually to the story's peril) include what I call a *scattered climactic scene*, but the formula holds up in almost every story you'll encounter. The closer the screenwriter or storyteller sticks to the formula, the more the audience loves the story itself.

When Tom Cruise decided to make a sequel to his enormous box-office hit *Top Gun*, he might have created the most formulaic movie in the history of man. The result: a $1.46 billion box-office juggernaut, the highest-grossing movie of Tom Cruise's career.

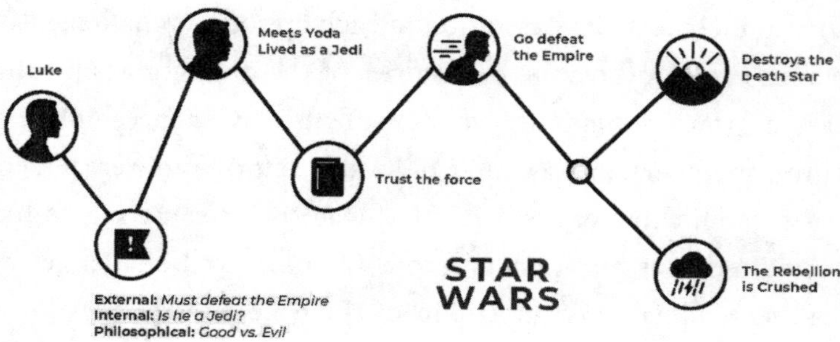

The fact that nearly every movie you go see at the theater includes all or most of the seven elements in the StoryBrand framework means the framework itself is something we should notice and respect. After thousands of years, storytellers the world over have arrived at this formula (or one like it) as a means of best practices. Simply put, this framework is the pinnacle of narrative communication. The further we veer away from these seven elements, the harder it becomes for audiences to engage. This is why indie films, which often break from narrative formulas, fail to gain critical acclaim and fail miserably at the box office. Critics sometimes like movies that disobey formulas, but that is because they are snobs who watch everything and are hungry for something different. The masses, who do not study movies professionally, want accessible stories that deliver entertainment.

Stories, by the way, don't have to be fictionalized to adhere to the formulas. One of my favorite documentary series is called *Welcome to Wrexham*, a true story about two Hollywood actors who bought a bottom-level soccer team in Wrexham, England, only to transform the team (and the town) from underdog losers into a fine-tuned winning machine. When the storytellers who produced the documentary series edited the story, they made sure to include a clear ambition in each episode, a challenge the heroes had to overcome, backstories of the protagonists (in this case a group protagonist story of townspeople, soccer players, family members, and a couple of lovable actors who were, essentially, humble but eager fish out of water) that caused us to like them, and tons and tons and tons of stakes and challenges all leading to (I hate to ruin it) skin-of-their-teeth victories. Wow. I think I lost two weeks of my life on the couch just clicking "next episode." I got so deep into it that my wife had to point out I was beginning to talk with a Welsh accent and kindly asked me to stop using soccer metaphors like "you really put this one in the back of the net" to describe her lovely outfit.

It seems true that some brands (as well as some screenwriters) break these formulas and succeed all the same, but when you look closely, this is rarely the case. Brilliant screenwriters know how to use the formula while still avoiding cliché. The same is true for brilliant marketers, by the way. The ability to keep it clear yet unique is what makes them brilliant. When you get good at the SB7 framework, hardly anybody will notice you are using it.

The Three Crucial Questions

So how do we make the story our company is telling clear?

Remember, the greatest enemy our business faces is the same enemy that good stories face: noise. Here's a good test to know whether the screenwriters are doing a good job keeping the story clear: at no point should you be able to pause a movie and fail to answer three critical questions.

1. What does the hero want?
2. Who or what is opposing the hero getting what they want?
3. What will the hero's life look like if they do (or do not) get what they want?

If you've ever started daydreaming in a movie, it was likely because your subconscious couldn't answer one of these questions, or worse, you didn't care. Here's the kicker: if these three questions can't be answered within the first fifteen to twenty minutes, the story has already descended into noise and will almost certainly fail its audience.

At StoryBrand, our certified coaches have reviewed thousands of pages of marketing copy that had nothing to do with the customer's story. We tell our clients the same thing my filmmaker friends told me when I was writing screenplays: anything that doesn't serve the plot has to go. Just because a tagline sounds great or a picture on a website grabs the eye doesn't mean it helps us enter into our customers' story. In every line of marketing and messaging copy we write, we're either serving the customer's story or descending into confusion; we're either making music or making noise.

Nobody remembers a company that makes noise.

DOES YOUR MARKETING PASS THE GRUNT TEST?

Just like there are three questions audiences must be able to answer to engage in a story, there are three questions potential customers must answer if we expect them to engage with our brand. And they should be able to answer these questions within five seconds of looking at our website or marketing material:

1. What do you offer?
2. How will it make my life better?
3. What do I need to do to buy it?

At StoryBrand, we call this *passing the grunt test*. The critical question is this: Could a caveman look at your website and immediately grunt your offer back to you?

Imagine a guy wearing a bearskin T-shirt, sitting in a cave by a fire, with a laptop across his lap. He's looking at your website. Would he be able to grunt an answer to the three questions posed above? If you were an aspirin company, would he be able to grunt, "You sell headache medicine, me feel better fast, me get it at Walgreens"? If not, you're likely losing sales.

Cut it with the cute copy that expensive ad agency charged you for. Nobody wants to go to your website and figure out a riddle. Just. Be. Clear.

CLARITY PRODUCES RESULTS

One of our early clients, Kyle Shultz, was a fireman in Ohio who looked into StoryBrand because he wanted to leave his job and pursue his passion of teaching photography. He had recently launched an online photography course aimed at parents. He'd worked hard to create terrific video training allowing moms everywhere to finally start using that basic camera they'd placed in the junk drawer because they felt it was too complicated. Interest was decent. In his first launch, he sold $25,000 worth of online courses. He was ecstatic. Still, it wasn't enough money for him to quit his job and pursue teaching photography full-time.

When Kyle encountered the SB7 framework, he began to wonder whether his message was too confusing. The night before his next launch he used the framework to completely rewrite his website. In fact, he removed 90 percent of the text he'd previously used on his sales page and stopped using inside language like "f-stop" and "depth of field." Instead, he used phrases like "Take those great pictures where the background is blurry."

The next day Kyle sent a mass email to the exact same email list he'd contacted only six months before and offered the course again. He wasn't expecting much because he'd already sold to this list, but to his surprise the course sold another $103,000 worth of registrations.

The difference? He highlighted the aspects of his course that would help parents survive and thrive (build stronger tribes, strengthen family connections, and connect more deeply with life's greater meaning), and he did so in such a simple way (with fewer than three hundred words on his sales page) that people didn't have to burn calories to figure out what was in it for them. Overnight, he'd gone from a cluttered mess to the clear guide in his customers' story.

Today, Kyle has quit his job and runs Shultz Photo School full-time. Every day he gets emails from parents thanking him for helping them feel great about the photographs they're taking of their children.

Here's another story: My wife made a friend named Nicole Burke. Her mission to make gardening ordinary was slowly gaining traction through her business, Gardenary. Nicole has a terrific, ready-for-television personality and has attracted a lot of clients. When she joined my mastermind and I reviewed her messaging collateral, I had to let her know that nobody wakes up wanting to make gardening ordinary. Her mission was just that: *her* mission. It wasn't her customers' mission. I told her to buy the domain StartAGarden.com because tons of people wake up on respective mornings and realize they want to start a garden. A quick Amazon.com and web search revealed nobody owned that idea. The mental real estate was wide open and she took it. Today, Nicole's business is poised to quadruple in revenue and influence, not because she launched a new product or because she got that television show (which she deserves) but because she started being clear. I believe Nicole is going to be a household name one day. Why? Because she is going to own a problem. If you want to start a garden, go see Nicole. The irony of her story is that by branding herself as the woman who can help you start a garden, she will make gardening ordinary, thus accomplishing her original mission. The moral: we will not accomplish our mission by explaining our own story; we will accomplish our mission by inviting customers into a story in which *they* can experience a clear win.

WE NEED A FILTER

Alfred Hitchcock defined a good story as "life with the dull parts taken out."[2] Good branding is the same. Our businesses are complex, for sure, but a good messaging filter will remove all the stuff that bores our customers and will accentuate the aspects of our brand that will help them survive and thrive.

So how do we come up with these messages? It's simple. We use a storytelling grid to map out a story our customers step into, then we create clear and refined statements in the seven relevant categories of their lives to position ourselves as their guides. When we do this, we become the people who help them overcome their challenges and achieve a life they want to live.

Once we begin filtering our message through the SB7 framework and using it as a communication filter, we will be able to repeat powerful messages over and over that "brand" us into our customers' lives.

The SB7 framework is simple, fun, and effective. And when you're done, your entire brand message is going to sit on a single sheet of paper. We call this single sheet of paper (actually, it's a free digital application I'm going to introduce you to) the StoryBrand BrandScript.

Once you've finished the process, you'll use your BrandScript to create all manner of improved messaging and marketing material, and you'll be more clearly positioned in the marketplace. Think of the StoryBrand framework as a weight-loss plan for messaging and marketing. When your messaging is lean and muscular, customers will finally start to listen. When customers understand how you can help them live a great story, your business will grow.

With that, let's take a look at the StoryBrand framework.

CHAPTER 3

THE SIMPLE SB7 FRAMEWORK

In the following chapters, I'll dive deep into the elements of the SB7 framework, showing you how each important category of messaging makes your brand more and more inviting to customers. You will use these seven categories to create powerful sound bites you can easily repeat over and over to get astonishing results. For now, though, let's take an overview so you can understand, in summary form, all that the StoryBrand framework can do to simplify your marketing and messaging.

THE STORYBRAND FRAMEWORK

1. A Character

StoryBrand Principle One: The customer is the hero, not your brand.

A major paradigm shift in the SB7 framework is that the customer is the hero of the story, not your brand. When we position our customer as the hero and ourselves as the guide, we will be recognized as a trusted resource to help our customers overcome their challenges.

Positioning the customer as the hero in the story is more than just good manners; it's also good business. However, it's counterintuitive. Communication expert Nancy Duarte has done extensive research on how to create powerful presentations. The strategy she recommends to her clients is simple: When giving a speech, position yourself as Yoda and your audience as Luke Skywalker.[1] This small but powerful shift honors the journey of the audience and positions us as a leader providing wisdom, products, and services they need in order to thrive.

In marketing and messaging, too many business leaders position themselves as the hero—and it's a turnoff. Imagine going to a movie in which the story stops so the screenwriter can come on screen to brag about how awesome the story is going and how brilliant they are at creating such great characters. No screenwriter would do that, would they? Yet business leaders do it all the time. Rather than invite their customers into a story, they talk about themselves, their mission, their goals, their backstory, and all sorts of stuff no customer cares about. Instead, let's understand our products from the customer's perspective.

Once we identify who our customer is, we have to ask ourselves what they want as it relates to our brand. The catalyst for any story is that the hero *wants something.* The rest of the story is a journey of discovering whether the hero will get what they want.

Unless we identify something our customer wants, they will never feel invited into the story we are creating. As we explore the first element of the StoryBrand framework, I'll show you what customers really want from your brand and how to invite them into a story that makes them pay attention to your brand so they can get what they want.

2. Has a Problem

StoryBrand Principle Two: The only things people buy are solutions to problems, and if you haven't identified your customer's problems or fail to talk about them clearly, you aren't going to sell anything.

In its purest form, a story starts with a character who lives in peace and stability. Suddenly that stability is disrupted: a bomb goes off, someone is kidnapped, or a disaster strikes. This sets up the start of the story, a predicament I call *the hero in a hole.* Once your hero is in a hole, the story begins, which, of course, is all about getting the hero out of the hole. The hero then sets out on a journey to return to the peaceful life they once enjoyed.

Customers are attracted to our brands for the same reason heroes are pulled into stories: They want to solve a problem that has, in big or small ways, disrupted their peaceful life. In short, every one of our customers is a "hero in a hole" looking for a way out. Whether they are looking for the perfect Mother's Day gift, relief from a headache, whiter teeth, a larger car to fit their growing family, or an investment that doubles as a tax break, your customers are in a hole and are looking for a way out. If we sell lawn-care products, our customers are coming to us because they're embarrassed about their lawn or they simply don't have time to do the work. If we sell financial advice, they're coming to us because they're worried about their retirement plan. It may not be as dramatic or sexy as James Bond going to Q to grab the latest high-tech spy weapon, but the premise is the same: our customers are in trouble and need our help.

By talking about the problems our customers face, we deepen their interest in everything we offer.

What most brands miss, however, is that there are three levels of problems a customer encounters. In stories, heroes encounter external, internal, and philosophical problems. Why? Because these are the same three levels of problems human beings face in their everyday lives. Almost all companies try to sell solutions to external problems, but as we unfold the StoryBrand framework, you'll see why customers are much more motivated to resolve their inner frustrations.

In the second element of the StoryBrand framework, we'll look at the three levels of problems our customers experience and create messages offering to resolve those problems. Understanding and addressing the three levels of problems our customers face will help us create a brand promise that will connect with customers on a primitive level and at their deepest point of need. This, in turn, will help us endear customers and create passionate brand evangelists.

3. And Meets a Guide

StoryBrand Principle Three: Customers aren't looking for another hero; they're looking for a guide.

If heroes in a story could solve their own problems, they would never get into trouble in the first place. That's why storytellers, through the centuries, have created another character to help the hero win. Depending on the scholar you talk to, there are many names for this character, but the term we use at StoryBrand is *the guide*.

In Tom Hooper's Academy Award–winning film *The King's Speech*, King George VI struggles to overcome a debilitating stutter. As Britain prepares for war against Germany, the Brits look to their leader for confidence and direction. Desperate, King George VI solicits the help of Lionel Logue, a dramatist turned speech therapist, who gives him a plan, coaches him to competency, and helps him transform into a powerful orator. This emotional and strategic support are the same service Obi-Wan (and Yoda) offers Luke Skywalker in *Star Wars*, Haymitch offers Katniss in *The Hunger Games*, Bing Bong offers Joy in Pixar's *Inside Out*, and countless other guides offer countless other heroes in nearly all our favorite stories.

It's no accident that guides show up in almost every narrative you encounter. Nearly every human being is looking for a guide (or guides) to help them win the day.

To position yourself as a hero is a mistake. Brands that position themselves as *heroes* unknowingly complicate their relationship with potential customers. Every human being wakes up each morning and sees the world through the lens of a protagonist. The world revolves around them, regardless of how altruistic, generous, and selfless a person they may be. Each day is, quite literally, about how *we* encounter our world. Potential customers feel the same way about themselves. They are the center of their world.

When a brand comes along and positions itself as the hero, customers remain distant. They hear us talking about how great our business is and subconsciously believe we're competing with them for scarce resources. Their subconscious thought pattern goes like this: *Oh, this is another hero, like me. I wish I had more time to hear their story, but right now I'm busy looking for a guide to get me out of this hole.*

Many brands have wrecked their potential by playing the hero instead of the guide. Many politicians have lost their elections because they positioned themselves as the hero instead of the guide. Many products have flopped upon launch, not because the product was bad but because the product itself was not positioned as a tool the hero could use to get out of their hole. These are fatal mistakes and, sadly, they are made all the time. As we explore the third element of the StoryBrand framework, we'll look at two mental triggers that will position you, your brand, and your products as the guide with the resources your customers have been looking for.

4. Who Gives Them a Plan

StoryBrand Principle Four: Customers trust a guide who gives them a plan.

At this point in our customers' story we've identified what they want, defined three levels of problems they're encountering, and positioned ourselves as their guide. And our customers love us for the effort. But they still aren't going to make a purchase. Why? Because we haven't laid out a simple plan of action they can take to get out of their hole.

Making a purchase is a huge step, especially if our products or services are expensive or time-consuming to adopt. What customers are looking for, then, is a clear path we've laid out that takes away any confusion they might have about how the process of getting out of the hole is going to work. The StoryBrand element we will use to create this path is called *the plan*.

In almost every story, the guide gives the hero a plan, usually in the form of a few steps they can take to get the job done. In the *Star Wars* movies, Yoda tells Luke to trust the Force and then trains him on how to wield this power. Lionel gives King George a series of exercises he can use to control his stutter in *The King's Speech*. The point is that people are looking for a philosophy they can embody or a series of steps they can take to solve their problems.

In the fourth element of the StoryBrand framework, we'll look at two kinds of plans: the agreement plan and the process plan. Each of these plans will earn trust and offer our customers a clear path to stability, effectively creating a ladder they can use to get out of their hole, greatly increasing the chance they will make a purchase.

5. And Calls Them to Action

StoryBrand Principle Five: Customers do not take action unless they are challenged to take action.

In stories, characters don't take action on their own. They must be challenged. If we're telling a story about a man who needs to lose thirty pounds and suddenly decides to do it of his own volition, the audience will be unable to suspend disbelief. Why? Because that's not how life works. There needs to be a reason our hero takes action. Our character has to run into a high school sweetheart who is now a yoga instructor, or he needs to lose a bet that forces him to run a marathon. In stories, heroes take action only after they are challenged by an outside force.

This principle is true in story because it's true in life. Human beings take action when their story challenges them to do so.

You would be surprised how many companies don't create obvious calls to action for their customers. They use phrases like "learn more" or "get started," which are more like passive-aggressive suggestions than clear calls to action. A call to action involves communicating a clear and direct step our customer can take to overcome their challenge and return to a peaceful life. Without clear calls to action, people will not engage our brand.

In the fifth part of the StoryBrand framework, I'll show you two calls to action that have worked for thousands of our clients. One call to action is direct, asking the customer for a purchase or to schedule an appointment. The other is a transitional call to action, furthering our relationship with the customer so we can continue to earn trust until they are ready to place an order. This changed my life forever and more than quadrupled the revenue of my own company when I put it into practice. Once we begin using both kinds of calls to action in our messaging, customers will understand exactly what we want them to do and will decide whether to let us play a role in their story. Until we call our customers to action, they will be inclined to ignore us, but when we call them to action (the right way), they will engage and place orders.

6. That Helps Them Avoid Failure

StoryBrand Principle Six: Every human being is trying to avoid a tragic ending to their story.

Stories sizzle or fizzle based on a single question: What's at stake? If nothing can be gained or lost, nobody cares. Will the hero disarm the bomb, or will people be killed? Will the hero get the girl, or will he be lonely and filled with self-doubt? These are the desired stakes being weighed in the minds of a story-hungry audience, and if we fail to include them, the audience quickly loses interest.

If there is nothing at stake in a story, there is no story. Likewise, if there's nothing at stake in whether I buy your product, I'm not going to buy your product. After all, why should I?

Simply put, we must show people the cost of *not* doing business with us.

In the eighties, the fast-food chain Wendy's effectively asked America, "Where's the beef?" The implication was that their competitors weren't using enough meat. So what's at stake for choosing another brand over Wendy's? We might get stuck with a wimpy sandwich. Likewise, Whole Foods has built an enormous industry helping customers avoid the consequences of overly processed foods, and Trader Joe's flourishes by helping customers avoid the consequences of Whole Foods' prices. All health food products are sold based on the stakes of un-health, feeling tired, shortened longevity, and so on. When inviting customers into a story, stakes matter.

Brands that help customers avoid some kind of negativity in

life (and clearly define what that negativity is by using plain language) engage them for the same reason good stories captivate an audience: they define what's at stake.

As we explore the sixth element of the StoryBrand framework, I'll help you identify what's at stake in your customers' story as it relates to your brand. Before we move on, though, it's important to note that by talking about your customers' problems and by painting the negative stakes, you will not come off as negative. As I've worked with thousands of brands to incorporate the framework, they are often concerned their brand will come off as pessimistic and sour. If this is a concern for you, know that the deeper the hole your hero transcends, the more powerful and positive the perceived outcome. If you fail to paint the negative stakes, you're essentially saying the hole your customer is in is not that deep, which cheapens the perceived value of your brand to rescue them. In other words, all negativity becomes positivity the moment the negativity is overcome. In element six, I will help you talk about the negative stakes your hero customers may encounter in such a way that they will think of you in the most positive light possible.

7. And Ends in a Success

StoryBrand Principle Seven: Never assume people understand how your brand can change their lives for the better. Tell them.

We must tell our customers how great their life can look if they buy our products and services. Ronald Reagan painted a picture of "a shining city on a hill."[2] Bill Clinton offered to help us "build a bridge to the twenty-first century."[3] During the dark and dreary Depression, Franklin Roosevelt used the song "Happy Days Are Here Again" as his official campaign song.[4] Likewise, Apple provides tools that allow us to express ourselves and be heard, Weight Watchers helps us lose weight and feel great, and Men's Wearhouse guarantees we will like the way we look. In essence, each of these brands lets potential customers (or voters) know what their lives can look like once they get out of their hole.

Think of it this way: everybody wants to be taken somewhere, and if we fail to tell people where we are capable of taking them, they will engage another brand.

In the seventh element of the StoryBrand framework, I'll elaborate on a critical sound bite to round out your messaging strategy: offering a vision for how great a customer's life could be if they engage your products or services. What sort of positive messages work? We will explore this and more in element seven.

WHEN YOU FEEL CONFUSED, CLARIFY YOUR MESSAGE

Right about now your head may be spinning. Even though there are only seven elements to the framework, how do we narrow down our message so our marketing and messaging material gets results?

We've created a tool to simplify the process. This tool is going to reduce the hassle of creating a clear message, save you time, entertain you as you use it, and motivate you to create messaging material that works. As I mentioned earlier, this tool is called the StoryBrand BrandScript, and it's going to become your new best friend.

Not only this, but we've updated the StoryBrand BrandScript to include AI prompts that will allow you to not only generate better sound bites but expand those sound bites into full messaging and marketing campaigns you can use to invite customers into a story. Nearly a million people have used the BrandScript tool in its old form, and now we've expanded its capability and look forward to hearing even more stories of outstanding results. The BrandScript is completely free for you as a bonus for purchasing this book.

You can create your StoryBrand BrandScript and subsequent messaging and marketing campaign at StoryBrand.AI, and it looks like this:

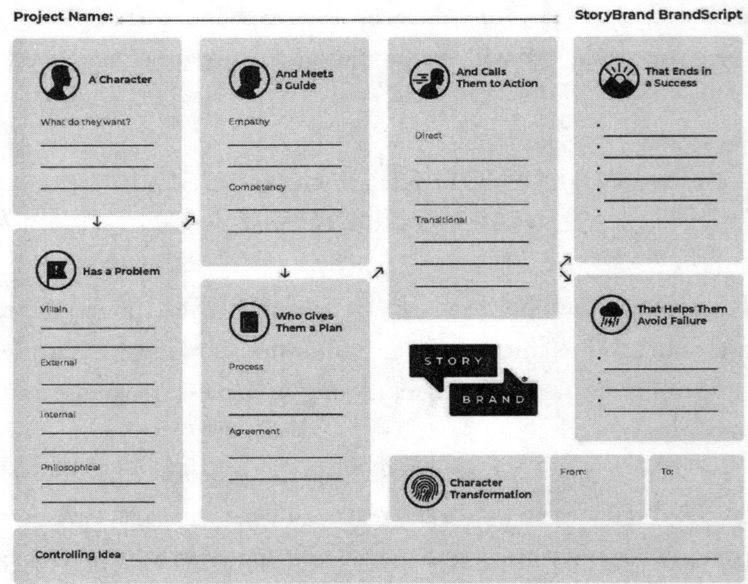

In the next seven chapters, I'm going to walk you through these seven elements of the framework and help you create your BrandScript. Your BrandScript will then reveal a series of short, simple sound bites you can use in all matter of messaging and marketing, including websites, keynote addresses, lead generators, digital and traditional advertising, and even casual conversation. You will find that when you create your sound bites and use them, your brand will gain more and more traction, and the more often you repeat them, the more you will succeed. Once you've created your sound bites, you'll no longer feel confused about how to talk about your products and services, and you'll have messages you can count on to powerfully engage potential customers.

The first project you should BrandScript is the one that represents your overall brand. Next you'll want to create a BrandScript for each division of your company, and after that, each product within each division. If you like, you can even create a BrandScript for each segment of your customer base. The uses for a StoryBrand BrandScript are endless. In fact, I used the StoryBrand BrandScript to outline this book and then used even more BrandScripts to write each chapter.

If you want to say it clearly, create a StoryBrand BrandScript.

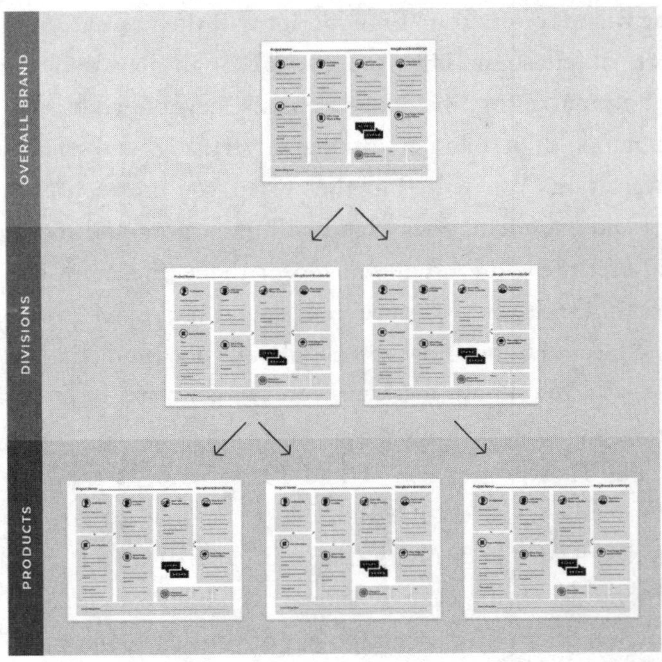

Again, to create a BrandScript you can save, edit, and come back to over and over, go to StoryBrand.AI.

Creating a StoryBrand BrandScript will do more than create a clear message you can use to engage customers; it will also give you clarity about the value you offer to the world. Many business leaders know their products are important but aren't exactly sure why. This confusion can create a lack of confidence about what you have created or what you represent. When you create a BrandScript, you will have much more confidence that what you do matters to the world.

CLARIFY YOUR MESSAGE SO CUSTOMERS LISTEN

As you walk through the seven elements of the StoryBrand framework, simply follow these three steps:

1. Read each of the next seven chapters.
2. After you read each chapter, brainstorm potential messages you might use to populate your BrandScript.
3. Carefully look at your brainstorm and then decide on a specific message to use in each section of your BrandScript.

Remember: simple, clear messages that are relevant to your customers result in sales.

Every human being is already fluent in storytelling, so when you begin using the SB7 framework, you'll finally be speaking their language.

THE STAKES ARE HIGH

You're going to be tempted to move ahead and skip thinking deliberately about each of the seven elements of the framework. You've already got the BrandScript, after all, so why not just fill it out?

Amateur screenwriters make the same mistake. They think they know how a story works, so they start typing and a couple of months later can't figure out why their story is boring or unrelatable. I'll tell you why. They had an overview of the process but never bothered to learn the actual rules.

Each module of the SB7 framework has set-in-stone rules you cannot break—or else customers won't find themselves in the story you're telling and will be much less likely to engage your brand.

Thousands of companies shut their doors every year, not because they don't have a great product but because potential customers can't figure out how that product will make their lives better. If we don't closely analyze each element of our customers' story, they'll sense we don't care and will move on to a competing brand that took the time to do the work.

Some of you are probably thinking it's too late. I mean, if it's printed in a book, everybody else is probably doing it. But are they? How many people read the first twenty pages of a book and then stop reading? I'd say most, which means you're already ahead of them. What would happen if you committed to executing this process and your competitor didn't? You'd win, wouldn't you? And how many people are actually going to put in the work even if they do read the book? Believe me, human nature tends toward complacency. Finish this process. Beat the competition. Clarify your message. Grow your business. The competition may be even more talented than you are, but they will never outwork you if you don't let them. That's the one thing you get to control.

In the next seven chapters, I'll show you how to create a clear and compelling message that will organize your thoughts, simplify your marketing, and grow your company.

SECTION 2

BUILDING YOUR STORYBRAND

When you're confused, create a StoryBrand BrandScript.

CHAPTER 4

A CHARACTER

StoryBrand Principle One: The customer is the hero, not your brand.

A story doesn't begin until the hero wants something. To engage the audience, the hero will need to disarm a bomb, win someone's heart, defeat a villain, or fight for their emotional or physical survival. Until it is clear what the hero wants, the audience is left waiting for "the story to get started." Once the storyteller defines what the hero wants, the question becomes, Will the hero get what she wants? And it's this single question that drives what I call *narrative traction.*

Positing the overall story question is why screenwriters have to define the character's ambition within the first nine or so minutes of a film. Will the underdog get the promotion? Will the runner finish the marathon? Will the team win the championship? These are the questions that can keep an audience engaged for hours on end.

If we want customers to engage our brand the way they engage their favorite movie, we, too, must define something the customer wants and must become known for delivering that thing and delivering it well. As soon as we define something our customer wants, we posit a series of story questions in the mind of the customer: *Can this brand really help me get what I want? If so, how much does it cost, where do I get it, and how soon can they ship it to me?* And what do they need to do to answer those questions? They need to buy our product.

Recently a high-end resort hired us to help them clarify their message. Like many companies, they were experiencing an identity crisis. Their marketing collateral featured images of their restaurant, front desk, and staff. It all looked nice, but unless they were trying to sell their buildings and their desk and their team, they weren't exactly inviting customers into a story.

What their customers wanted most, actually, was a luxurious, restful experience. After StoryBranding their resort, they changed the text on their website from long stories about themselves (which positioned them as the hero rather than the customer) to images of a warm bath, plush towels and robes, someone getting a massage in the spa, and a looping clip of a back porch rocking chair against the backdrop of trees blowing in the wind along a golf course.

They replaced the text on their main page with short and powerful copy: "Find the luxury and rest you've been looking for." That became the controlling idea that defined the culture for the entire staff too. This phrase was posted on their office walls, and to this day you can stop any team member, from the sous chef to the groundskeeper, and they will tell you their customers are looking for two things: luxury and rest. Defining exactly what their customer wanted brought clarity and camaraderie to the team because they understood their mission. Each member of the staff then understood his or her role in the story they were inviting their customers to engage in.

One university we worked with defined their customer's desire as "a hassle-free MBA you can complete after work." That may sound overly simple, but don't be fooled. Your brand will grow when people can easily remember what you offer, and people don't remember complexity. A landscaping company humorously defined their customers' ambition as "a yard that looks better than your neighbor's." A caterer we worked with in Los Angeles defined his customers' desire as "a mobile fine-dining experience in the environment of your choice."

When we identify something our customer wants and communicate it simply, the story we are inviting them into is given definition and direction.

Here are some more examples from companies we've worked with:

Financial Adviser: "A Plan for Your Retirement"
College Alumni Association: "Leave a Meaningful Legacy"
Fine-Dining Restaurant: "A Meal Everybody Will Remember"
Real Estate Agent: "The Home You've Dreamed About"
Bookstore: "A Story to Get Lost In"
Breakfast Bars: "A Healthy Start to Your Day"

When you define something your customers want, they are invited to direct their story in your direction. And if they see your brand as a trustworthy and reliable guide and believe you can deliver on your promise, they are likely to engage.

OPEN A STORY GAP

Identifying a potential desire your customer can fulfill opens what, in storyteller terms, is called a *story gap*. The idea is you place a gap between your hero and what they want. Moviegoers pay attention when there's a story gap because they wonder if and how the gap is going to be closed.

Jason Bourne is a spy who has amnesia, and we wonder if he'll ever discover his true identity. He then finds out who he really is, which closes the gap, only for another gap to open when he wants to escape the agency that is trying to kill him. While that story gap is open, another story gap opens when he meets a young woman named Marie (enter love story subplot), and as they get together, that gap closes, only for yet another to open. Bourne and Marie have to flee the country. When they escape, that gap closes as yet another one opens. The cycle goes on and on, maintaining a taut grip on the audience's attention up until the finale.

Here's a storytelling rule that you can immediately apply to your business: attention rises and lowers with the opening and closing of a story gap.

For instance, recently I spoke to an audience of gift retailers. Because Mother's Day was coming up, I advised the audience to open and close a story gap to drive sales. First, I told them to place a sign on the sidewalk outside the store that said, "Looking for something Mom will love for Mother's Day? We've got 20 ideas under $100." Then, in the store itself, I instructed them to place respectively numbered cards on twenty items around the store with the language: "#17 Mom Is Going to Love This." The result? The stores reported significant increase in sales on all the numbered items. Why? Because the sign on the sidewalk opened a story gap and the numbered cards inside the store offered to close that gap. This simple strategy could be repeated for Valentine's Day, Christmas, Father's Day, the Fourth of July, Easter, anniversaries, and on and on and on. In fact, a simple-to-produce promotion like this could be orchestrated nearly every month.

To understand the power of a story gap is to understand what compels a human brain toward a desire. And it's not just cinematic or literary stories. Even classical music follows the formula of the opening and closing of story gaps. Many classical sonatas can be broken into three sections: exposition, development, and recapitulation. The final section, recapitulation, is simply an altered version of the exposition that brings a sense of resolve. If that doesn't make sense, try singing "Twinkle, Twinkle, Little Star" without singing the final note on the word *are*. It will bother you to no end.

We also see this at work in poetry. When our ears hear Lord Byron's first line "She walks in beauty, like the night," a story gap has been opened. We are waiting to hear a word that rhymes with *night* and closes the open gap in our minds. Once we hear "Of cloudless climes and starry skies," our minds find a bit of resolution. Until the next line, that is.

Even a good dad joke follows the opening and closing of a story gap. Opening the gap: A man accidentally ran over his neighbor's cat and agonizingly apologized, saying he would certainly replace the cat if the neighbor wished. Closing the gap: The neighbor replied: "I'm not so sure about that. How good are you at catching mice?"

It is my view that story gaps explain a lot more than how and why we pay attention. They also explain *all* of human behavior. The opening of a story gap works a magnetic force that drives every action we take and certainly every dollar we spend. Hunger is the opening of a story gap, and lunch is how we close that gap. A headache is the opening of a story gap, and aspirin is what we take to make it go away. Arousal is the opening of a story gap,ambition

and sexual fulfillment brings its closing. There is little action in life that can't be explained by the opening and closing of various story gaps.

The business lesson here is that when we fail to define something our customer wants, we fail to open a story gap in their mind. When we fail to open a story gap in our customer's mind, we give them no motivation to engage our brand because they are not left with a story question that demands resolution. Defining something our customer wants and featuring it in our messaging and marketing will open a story gap that drives engagement and action.

PARE DOWN THE CUSTOMER'S AMBITION TO A SINGLE FOCUS

A critical mistake many organizations make in defining something their customers want is not paring down that desire to a single focus. I've had countless conversations with frustrated business leaders who push back at this point and say, "Wait, we provide about twenty-seven things our customers want, and we talk about all of them, but sales remain flat."

My answer to them is this: You're off to a good start, but listing too many benefits often backfires. Human beings cannot hold large amounts of new information in their heads at once. If you want to grow your brand (or write a good screenplay), define a single desire you are able to fulfill and then add to that desire in subsequent marketing and messaging. The objective is this: Define a specific desire your customers have and become known for helping people achieve that specific desire. If you try to open too many story gaps at once, your audience will become confused about what, exactly, you offer.

Paring down your offering can be frustrating if your products and services fulfill many desires. The reality of a diverse brand, though, brings the same challenge many amateur screenwriters succumb to: they clutter the story by diluting their hero's desire with too many ambitions. If Jason Bourne wants to know who he is and also lose thirty pounds and marry his high school sweetheart and finish a marathon and perhaps adopt a cat, we've ruined the story because the audience will have to burn too many mental calories trying to figure out what this story is about.

As you create a BrandScript for your overall brand, focus on one simple desire your customer has and then, as you create campaigns for each division and maybe even each product, you can identify more things your customer wants in the subplots of your overall StoryBrand.

In the following grid, you'll get a picture of what a diverse brand might look like using the tool of various StoryBrand BrandScripts.

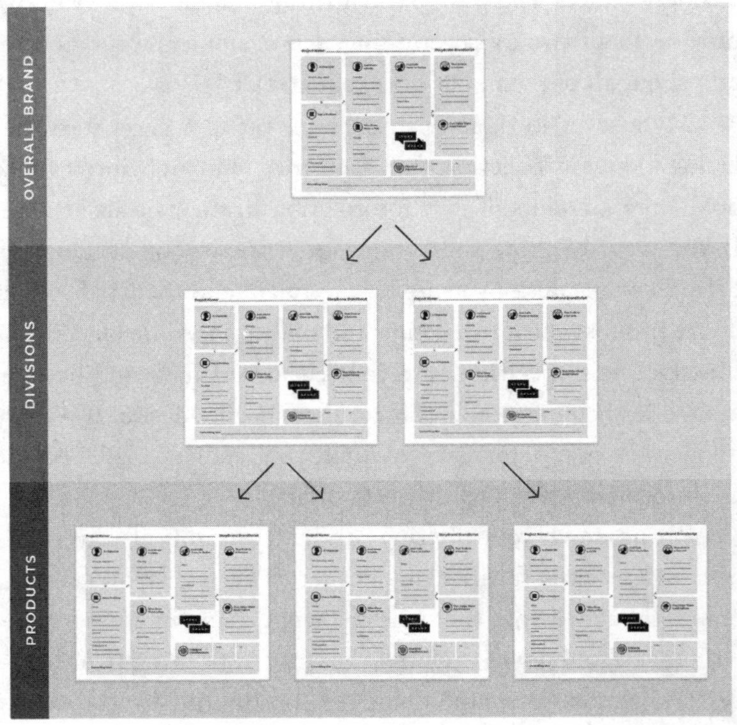

At the highest level, the most important challenge for business leaders is to define something simple and relevant their customers want and to become known for delivering on the promise. Everything else is a subplot that, after having delivered on the customer's basic desire, will only serve to delight and surprise them all the more.

CHOOSE A DESIRE RELEVANT TO THE CUSTOMER'S SURVIVAL

Once a brand defines what their customer wants, they are often guilty of making the second mistake: what they've defined isn't related to the customer's survival. In their desire to cast a wide net, brands define a blob of a desire that is so vague, potential customers can't figure out why they need it in the first place.

A leadership expert recently asked for feedback on his brand. As I reviewed his marketing material, I noticed he was making a critical mistake: he was vague when defining what his customer wanted.

The idea behind his brand is that he imparts knowledge to potential leaders. He saw himself as a storehouse of leadership resources and wanted to be the go-to guy for achieving excellence. In fact, his tagline was "Inhale Knowledge, Exhale Success."

Seems clear enough, but is it? What does exhaling success even mean? He was making potential customers burn too many mental calories to figure out how he was going to help them survive and thrive.

I recommended he make an edit to his message. Instead of saying, "Inhale Knowledge, Exhale Success," simply say, "Helping You Become Everyone's Favorite Leader."

Becoming everyone's favorite leader means the customer would be more respected and better connected to a tribe, they'd have greater social and career opportunities, and much more. Exhaling success sounded nice, but thriving as the leader of a tribe is directly connected to survival. People will always choose a story that helps them survive and thrive.

Fortunately, he liked the idea, mostly because that's what he was already doing. Defining something the customer wants (to be a respected leader) and connecting it with the customer's desire for survival (respect within a tribe) opened an enticing story gap for potential clients and, of course, coaching inquiries went up.

What Does Survival Mean?

When I say *survival*, I'm talking about that primitive desire we all have to be safe, healthy, happy, and strong. Survival simply means we have the physical, economic, and social resources to eat, drink, reproduce, and fend off foes.

So what kinds of desires fit under this definition? Well, too many to count, but consider these examples:

Conserving financial resources. In order to survive and thrive, your customers may need to conserve resources. In simple terms, this means they may need to save money. If your brand can help them save money, you've tapped into a survival mechanism. Walmart has built their brand on the promise of everyday low prices. Their tagline "Save Money. Live Better" further communicates savings and value and thus taps into a basic function of survival, the conservation of resources. Does it work? Even with terrifyingly low profit margins, Walmart remains one of the largest companies in the world.

Conserving time. In developed countries, most of our customers have thankfully moved beyond the hunter-gatherer stage of survival. They are familiar, then, with the notion of opportunity costs. Can your housecleaning service give your customers more time to work on other things or more time to spend with family? Then they might be interested. Michael Hyatt's *Full Focus Planner*, one of the most successful day planning systems of all time, has earned the respect of millions by offering users the invaluable gift of time.

Building social networks. If our brand can help people find community, we've tapped into yet another survival mechanism. We think we're only being nice when we bring our coworkers coffee, but what if we're actually being nice because our primitive brains want to make connections in an effort to build a tribe in case the bad guys come knocking at the door? Add this to the fact human beings have a strong desire to nurture and be nurtured, and we've tapped into yet another survival mechanism. The Coach Builder Community has flourished by offering coaches the chance to build community with each other, sharing best practices and encouragement. So has every church, every sports league, every Alcoholics Anonymous chapter, every Girl Scout troop, and countless other examples of organizations and institutions that lead with the offer of community.

Gaining status. Luxury brands like Mercedes and Rolex don't make much practical sense in terms of survival, right? In fact, spending lots of money buying a luxury car when a more common brand would do the trick seems counter to our survival, doesn't it? Not when you consider the importance of status. Gaining status, in any tribe, is a survival strategy. Status projects a sense of abundance that may attract powerful allies, repel potential foes (just as a lion by using a loud roar), and, if we're into shallow companions, even help us secure a mate. Rolex, Mercedes, Louis Vuitton, and other luxury brands are truly selling more than just cars and watches; they're selling an identity associated with power, prestige, refinement, and, yes, survival.

Accumulating resources. If the products and services you offer help people make money or accumulate much-needed resources, that will quickly translate into a person's desire for survival. With more money, our customers will have more opportunity to secure many of the other survival resources they may need. Many StoryBrand clients run business-to-business offerings (StoryBrand itself is a business-to-business company), so offering increased productivity, increased revenue, or decreased waste are powerful associations with the need for a business (or an individual) to survive and thrive. Every financial adviser on the planet sells the accumulation of resources (that is, if they are smart).

Showing generosity. None of the desires I've listed are evil. They can all be taken too far, but the reality is we are designed to survive. Still, we should be comforted by the fact that nearly all human beings have an enormous potential for generosity. Achieving an aspirational identity of being sacrificial actually helps us survive (fends off foes, decreases outside criticism, helps earn trust in our tribe, and so on), but it also taps into something truly redemptive: we want other people to survive too. Most people are not nearly as Darwinian in their thinking as we've been led to believe. We are empathetic and caring creatures who will gladly sacrifice for the well-being of others, often in anonymity. The truth is we aren't only interested in our own survival; we're interested in the survival of others. Especially those who have not been given the opportunities we enjoy. Another consideration, especially for those in the nonprofit space, is that by being generous, our donors are actually increasing their own chance of survival. Why does the NFL constantly associate with soft and tender charitable efforts? Because, while certainly being a generous brand, they are smart: they're softening the image of a violent sport, thus executing on a strategy that helps the brand itself survive.

Desiring meaning. Viktor Frankl was right when he contended with Sigmund Freud, insinuating that the chief desire of man is not pleasure but meaning. In fact, in his book *Man's Search for Meaning*, Frankl argued convincingly that man was actually most tempted to distract himself with pleasure when his life was void of meaning.[1] So how do we offer potential customers a sense of meaning? Not unlike giving our customers the opportunity to be generous, we invite them to participate in something greater than themselves. A movement. A cause to champion. A valiant fight against a real villain, be that villain flesh and blood or a harmful philosophy. The clothing brand Patagonia has made a name for itself through its altruistic business model, turning down millions in profit in their commitment to sustainable corporate practices. Their effort is a grand example of meaning over money, which (rightly so) has rewarded them in financial strength through a devoted customer base who also wants their clothes to be something more than just warm and fashionable.

WHAT'S THE STORY QUESTION YOU ARE POSING TO YOUR CUSTOMER?

When I offered my executive coach friend the tagline "Helping You Become Everyone's Favorite Leader," his customers' brains were able to translate that message into multiple survival categories, including a social network, status, the innate desire to be generous, the opportunity to gain resources, and even the desire for deeper meaning.

In business, if we don't communicate clearly, we shrink. When we're motivating a team, convincing shareholders to stay engaged, or selling to customers, we must define a desire our customers have or we will fail to open a story gap and the audience we desire will ignore us. Remember, customers want to envision the great place you are going to take them. Unless you identify something they want, it's doubtful they will follow you.

Imagine your customer is a hitchhiker. You pull over to give him a ride, and the one burning question on his mind is simply this: *Where are you going?* But as he approaches, you roll down the window and start talking about your mission statement, or how your grandfather built this car with his bare hands, or how your road trip playlist is all 1980s alternative. This person doesn't care. All he wanted was to get to San Francisco with a flower in his hair.

The goal for our branding should be that every potential customer knows exactly where we will take them: to visit a luxury resort where they can get some rest, to become the leader everybody loves, or to save money and live better. One of my favorite clothing brands, Filson, makes high-quality clothes and gear for what I think of as the upscale outdoors. They've been in business for over a hundred years, and just wearing their shirts and pants makes me feel like I've stepped back in time to when things were just made better. When I think about a brand that makes me feel that way, however, I wonder how those thoughts got in my head in the first place. To be sure, their clothing looks and feels great, but there are many brands that compete on quality. Where did I get the idea that they were the best? It turns out they told me. It's right there on the Filson tag, right next to the size of the shirt. "Might as well have the best" is printed on most of their items. Smart. Don't assume your customers know what you are offering. Tell them. And tell them in plain, simple, and repeatable language. The only way word will get out about your brand is if you give people the exact words to use.

If you randomly asked a potential customer where your brand wants to take them, would they be able to answer? Would they be able to repeat back to you exactly what your brand offers? If not, your brand is suffering the cost of confusion. You can fix this. Define a desire your customer base has and start talking about it. When you do, the story you are inviting customers into will have a new and powerful hook.

CLARIFY YOUR MESSAGE SO CUSTOMERS LISTEN

- Go to StoryBrand.AI and either create a StoryBrand BrandScript or log in to your existing BrandScript.
- Either alone or with a team, brainstorm what potential desires your customers might have that you can fulfill.
- Make a decision. Choose something your customer wants and fill in the "character" module of your StoryBrand BrandScript.
- Read the next chapter and repeat this process for the next section of your BrandScript.

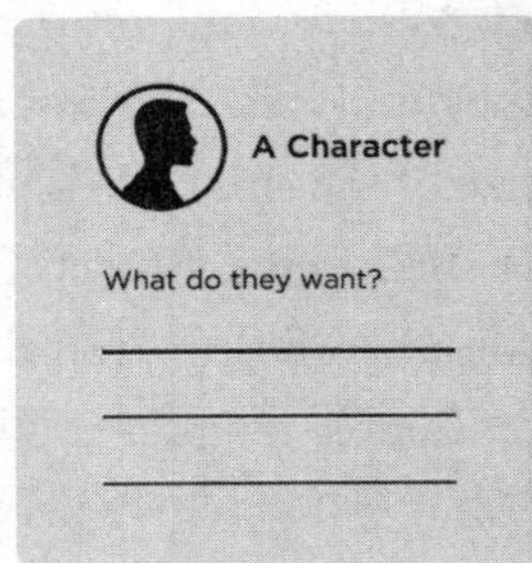

Once you fill out the first module of your StoryBrand BrandScript, you'll be on your way to inviting customers into an incredible story. At this point, they're interested in you and what you offer. But what can we do to entice them even further into a story? Let's move on to the next StoryBrand element and find out!

You will be tempted to fill out the rest of your StoryBrand BrandScript now, but I encourage you to read the chapter associated with each StoryBrand element to be sure you're filling it out correctly. Once you've completed your first BrandScript, section 3 of this book will help you create simple, effective marketing and messaging tools.

CHAPTER 5

HAS A PROBLEM

StoryBrand Principle Two: Companies tend to sell solutions to external problems, but customers buy solutions to internal problems.

Now that you've piqued your potential customers' curiosity about your brand, how do you deepen their interest so that they are more likely to place an order? You borrow yet another play from the storyteller's playbook; you start talking about the problems your customers are living with because they don't have your product yet.

Identifying our customers' problems deepens their interest in the story we are inviting them into because when we identify their problem, we open the story gap even wider.

In a story, the problem is the "hook," and if we don't identify our customers' problems, the story we are inviting them into will fizzle fast. Until our hero has a problem, the story fails to gain traction, and as soon as the conflict in a story is resolved, audiences stop paying attention. The next time you watch a movie, pause the screen at any point and I promise you will be able to identify a problem the hero is dealing with. Even if you are watching a documentary, the same principle applies. Documentary filmmakers must identify a problem in each section because if they don't, the documentary will fail.

In fact, there's a parlor trick I often play in my home when I'm making this point. Our carriage house doubles as a library and contains over a thousand books. When I talk about how every story is about problems being solved, I ask somebody to go to the shelf and pull out any book. When they do, I ask them to open the book to any page, then I ask them to set their finger down on any paragraph. Once this is done I let them know what that paragraph is about. It's about conflict. It's about a problem. It's about a hero who is up against trouble and is fighting their way out. And you know what? I've never been wrong. Why is nearly every sentence in every novel about conflict? Because a good writer knows that conflict is how you get people's attention. This is also why every politician wants their constituents to believe the country is going to hell in a hand basket. If it weren't, why would anybody need them? The same is true of the news. When is the last time you turned on the news to discover everything was going great? No news program will ever admit things are okay, because if they did, you'd go outside and fly a kite with your kids and they'd be out of a job.

Certainly there are constant problems happening in the world, but are they nearly as bad as the media would have us believe? Not at all. As the novelist James Scott Bell says, "Readers want to fret."[1]

As careful as we must be to refrain from manipulating people with half-truths and exaggerations, those of us who build brands can learn a thing or two from professionals in the entertainment industry (and I'd include twenty-four-hour news outlets as producers of entertainment). Conflict gets people's attention.

If Jason Bourne were to receive a call thirty minutes into *Bourne Identity* and on the other end of the call a gentle voice explained who Jason really was, why he'd suffered amnesia, and that the government was sorry for the offense and offering a pension along with a house on the coast, the moviegoing audience would lose interest because the *reason* to pay attention would be gone. If there is no conflict in the story, there is no story gap, and without a story gap, there is no reason to pay attention.

It bears repeating: the more we talk about the problems our customers experience, the more curiosity they will have about our brand.

So how do we put this idea to work in our messaging? It's simple. Figure out what problem your products solve. Are you a clothing boutique? Talk about how hard it is to find something to wear that goes with anything. Talk about how important it is to stand out in the office. Talk about how frustrating it is to find clothes that are well-made. When you talk about a problem, people become interested in finding a solution, which means you sell more of your products.

Last year I spent time with a powerful government agency to help them clarify messaging on foreign policy. I can't name the agency because of a nondisclosure agreement, but I can share the messaging points as they were always intended to be public facing from the beginning. In fact, it is hoped the talking points will be repeated by many, so I'm happy to do my part. As we spent the day together, filling whiteboards and keynote decks with talking point after talking point, I realized the nature of the threat against America, and I found the significant "problems" we were up against to be concerning, to say the least. The threat the agency wanted the public to understand was this: *A global force is taking shape to empower authoritarian regimes.* As I sat there looking at the whiteboard, I realized the threat my family faced, especially my young daughter, was significant. I confess that until it had been spelled out so clearly, I'd not paid much attention. With the help of the folks in that room, I realized there are significant forces threatening our democracy, our economy, and our culture. In short, the very idea of democracy is a threat to the personal power of some of the world's most authoritarian leaders. Specifically, if citizens under authoritarian regimes witness the peaceful transfer of power in America, along with economic and cultural freedom and flourishing, their people will want it too, which threatens the stranglehold the autocratic leader must maintain over their own people. Because of this, democracies *must* be diminished or destroyed on the world stage. Trillions of dollars, books filled with lies, rooms filled with hackers, and ships and planes loaded with weapons are all being utilized against America and all other successful democracies. Our job in that room was to find the right words to adequately warn a distracted American public, and it was certainly working on me.

HOW TO TALK ABOUT YOUR CUSTOMERS' PROBLEMS

In the second module of the StoryBrand framework, we're going to look at three elements of conflict that will increase customer interest, ratchet up engagement, and give a greater depth of meaning to the story our brand is inviting customers into.

First, though, let's start with the root of where all this conflict is coming from. I'm talking about one of the most dynamic, interesting characters in any story: the villain.

The Villain Gives the Problem a Root Cause and a Focus

The villain is the number one device storytellers use to give conflict a clear point of focus.

Screenwriters and novelists know the stronger, more evil, more dastardly the villain, the more sympathy we will have for the hero and the more the audience will want them to defeat their foe and return to their previous state of stability.

How much less sympathetic would Batman be if it weren't for the diabolical Joker? Would we root as strongly for Luke Skywalker if it weren't for the haunting presence of Darth Vader? Doesn't Harry Potter become infinitely more heroic under the threat of Voldemort? What about superman without the threat of Kryptonite? (Let's be honest, Lex Luthor isn't that interesting of a bad guy.)

Here's why this matters in the building of your brand: If we want our customers' ears to perk up when we talk about our products and services, we should position these as weapons they can use to defeat a villain. The more dastardly the villains, the more urgent their need for our products.

If we're selling time-management software, for instance, we might talk about time thieves, those people who want to steal our time by locking us in meetings in which nothing gets done, or coworkers who stand around the coffee machine waiting for the next victim they can capture for a long conversation about their latest Netflix find. That's a good villain. Now that we've identified the villain, we can talk about the conflict they stir up, that conflict being *distractions.* Our time-management software could then be offered as a weapon that stops time thieves in their tracks. After all, we have to get back to our "blocked for deep work" session. Time thieves could be personified as snipers in the woods, taking shots at us when we least expect it. When you use our new time-management system, however, you learn to say no to unimportant meetings and get-togethers, which keeps you out of the woods in the first place. Sounds kind of dramatic, right? Yet distractions are what's diluting our customers' potential, wrecking their families, stealing their sanity, and costing them enormous amounts of time and money. Time thieves, then, are a great personification of the villains and distractions our product helps people avoid. Don't be afraid of a little drama in your messaging, especially if that drama is true.

The point is, real threats exist in the world. If your customer wasn't experiencing some sort of pain or frustration as it relates to your brand, they wouldn't be seeking you out anyway. Take your customers' frustrations seriously. Whether we are talking about artery-blocking cholesterol, money-eating inflation, or sleep-disrupting anxiety, we are naive to assume our customers' quality of life isn't under threat. And if our product can protect our customers, we can and should name the villains out to get them.

Now that I've pointed out the technique of identifying villains in our customers' challenges, you'll see the messaging methodology being used in television commercials all the time. Who knew that those dust bunnies collecting along the baseboards of our houses move around in animated, criminal gangs wearing leather jackets, coordinating their devilish efforts to ruin our floors? Ah, that is, until they meet their match: the new mop from ACME Mop Company.

Advertisers personify the villains their customers face in order to capture their customers' imaginations and give their frustrations a focal point. Fuzzy hairballs with squeaky voices living in your drains, making nests, and clogging up the pipes? Yellow globs of living, breathing, talking plaque vacationing between your teeth? These are all personified versions of conflict. They're all villains.

Here are four characteristics that make for a good villain on your StoryBrand BrandScript:

1. **The villain should be a root source.** High taxes, for example, are not an example of a villain; they are what a villain makes us experience. Rather, the broken-down government is a good example of a villain that is charging us all that tax money to do precisely nothing but use it to collect salaries and stir up culture wars so they can get re-elected and continue their important work of doing nothing.
2. **The villain should be relatable.** When people hear us talk about the villain, they should immediately recognize it as something they disdain.
3. **The villain should be singular.** One villain is enough. A story with too many villains falls apart for lack of clarity.
4. **The villain should be real.** Never go down the path of being a fear-monger. There are plenty of actual villains out there to fight. Let's go after them on behalf of our customers.

5. **Another thing: the villain doesn't have to be serious.** If you're creating the messaging for the upcoming Boston Red Sox versus New York Yankees series, personifying your opponent as the villain is just smart marketing. Turning the opposition into a villain will fill the stands at either stadium and increase the urgency the audience feels while rooting for their team.

Is there a villain in your customers' story? Of course there is. What is the chief source of conflict that your products and services defeat? Talk about this villain. The more you do, the more people will want a tool to help them escape the villain's deadly grasp.

Later, when you're creating your BrandScript, I'll ask you to brainstorm what kind of villain your customer faces. For now, though, let's look closely at the kinds of conflict this villain causes. Once we understand the three levels of problems our customers encounter, we'll have a better idea of how to talk about their problems in such a way that they engage.

The Three Levels of Conflict

A villain is the antagonist because they cause the hero serious problems. That's obvious. But what's less obvious is that in a story, there are three levels of problems that work together to increase the urgency and draw the moviegoing audience further and further in.

The three levels of problems heroes (and customers) face are

- external problems,
- internal problems, and
- philosophical problems

In a story, a villain initiates an external problem that causes the character to experience an internal frustration that is, quite simply, philosophically wrong. These are also the three levels of problems a customer hopes to solve when they buy a product.

I know that sounds complicated, but let's take a closer look at each level of conflict so we know exactly how to talk about each frustration so that it is as intriguing as it can be.

EXTERNAL PROBLEMS

In literature, a villain's job is to wreak havoc on the hero, to place barriers between them and the stability they desire. But ill intentions aren't enough. Something, that is, some *thing* (or things) must represent this barrier. Enter the external problem.

In stories, the external problem is often a physical, tangible problem the hero must overcome in order to save the day. The problem might manifest itself as a ticking time bomb or a runaway bus, or maybe even a combination of the two: a bomb on a bus that will go off if Keanu Reeves doesn't keep the speed above fifty miles per hour!

The external problem works like a football set between the hero and the villain, and each is trying to gain control of it so they can win the game.

For Billy Beane in the movie *Moneyball*, the external problem is the need to win baseball games. For Matthew Broderick in the movie *WarGames*, it's a piece of rogue software that has taken over the American government's computer system and is waging a deadly war against the Soviets.

But what does the existence of an external problem in a story have to do with branding? Well, most of us are in the business of solving external problems. We provide insurance or clothes or soccer balls. If we own a restaurant, the external problem we solve is hunger. The external problem a plumber fixes might be a leaky pipe, just like a pest-control guy might solve the external problem of termites in the attic.

Brainstorming what external problems you solve will be the easiest part of creating your StoryBrand BrandScript. The external problem is usually obvious. But you'd be wrong to think the reason people call you, walk through your door, or visit your website is limited to the resolution of an external problem. Something else is going on.

INTERNAL PROBLEMS

By limiting our marketing messages to external problems, we neglect a principle that is costing us thousands and potentially millions of dollars. That principle is this: *companies tend to sell solutions to external problems, but people buy solutions to internal problems.*

The purpose of an external problem in a story is to manifest an internal problem. If I wrote a movie about a guy who simply needed to disarm a bomb, audiences would lose interest. What storytellers and screenwriters do, then, is create a backstory of frustration in the hero's life.

In the movie *Moneyball*, for instance, Billy Beane failed in his playing career and so was filled with self-doubt about whether he could redeem himself as a general manager. In *Star Wars*, Luke Skywalker was told by his uncle that he was too young to join the Rebellion, so he doubted his ability until the very end.

In almost every story the hero struggles with the same question: *Do I have what it takes?* This question can make them feel frustrated, incompetent, and confused. The sense of self-doubt is what makes a movie about baseball relatable to a soccer mom and a romantic comedy relatable to a truck-driving man.

Stories teach us that people's internal desire to resolve a frustration is a greater motivator than their desire to solve an external problem.

This is where most brands make a critical mistake. By assuming our customers only want to resolve external problems, we fail to engage the deeper frustration they're feeling. The truth is, it's those frustrations that are motivating them to call you.

The key to discovering your customers' internal problem is to ask yourself (or preferably, them) what the external problem they are dealing with is causing them to feel. For instance, if you sell childcare, the external problem is that the kids need a nanny, but what is this need causing your potential customers to feel? Helpless? Hopeless? Tired? Overwhelmed? These are the internal problems your customers are experiencing, and the more you talk about them, the more people want to buy your product so they can resolve those frustrations. When we ask, "What does this problem make our customers feel?" we can easily brainstorm great copy that will improve our marketing efforts.

After their near collapse, Apple didn't find their footing until Steve Jobs understood that people felt intimidated (internal problem) by computers and wanted a friendlier interface with technology. In one of the most powerful advertising campaigns in history, Apple showed a simple, hip, fun character who just wanted to take photos and listen to music and write books next to a not-so-hip tech nerd who wanted to talk about the inner workings of his operating system. The campaign positioned Apple Computers as the company to go to if you wanted to enjoy life and express yourself but felt marginalized by all the tech talk. In this specific campaign, Apple started selling more than computers; they sold a resolution to the problem of customer intimidation. Understanding their customers' internal problem is one of the reasons Apple experienced rapid growth and created passionate brand evangelists.

The only reason our customers buy from us is because their external problem is frustrating them in some way. If we can identify that frustration, put it into words, and offer to resolve it along with the original external problem, we do more than just sell our customers products; we bond with our customers because we've positioned ourselves deeply into their narrative.

For example, if we own a house-painting business, our customer's external problem might be an unsightly home. The internal problem, however, may involve a sense of embarrassment about having the ugliest house on the block. Knowing this, our marketing could offer "Paint That Will Make Your Neighbors Jealous."

One of our clients, Stephen Boice, recently incorporated more internal messaging on his website and saw an increase in business, just by changing a few words. Stephen and his wife own Vitality Aesthetics, a face and skin studio in Florida that offers over thirty different treatments to help their customers look better. The header at the top of their website previously read, "Your Natural Beauty" and featured a picture of an attractive woman being treated by an aesthetician. While the website looked great and business was strong, I asked David to try something slightly different: Add *get* and *back* to their header. In other words, instead of saying "Your Natural Beauty," say "Get Your Natural Beauty Back," knowing that as most of us get older and spend more time in the sun, we lose our youthful looks a little faster than we have to. By identifying a customer's *feeling* that they have lost something, David would be tapping into an internal frustration. I also asked David to include a price list that included all the procedures he offered but to give the price list away only in exchange for an email address. Once a potential customer downloaded the price list (definitely a qualified and interested customer), I asked him to send thirty emails over thirty weeks documenting how thirty separate clients felt about themselves after engaging each of his products. By creating an automated email campaign that taps into his customers' internal frustrations and tells stories of how other customers had been relieved of those frustrations, David began to grow his business again. As digital advertising becomes more expensive and less effective, adding sound bites to our messaging that speak to our customers' internal problems becomes more and more important as a way to generate greater engagement.

What Frustrations Do Our Products Resolve?

Recently, the rental car company National got my business by understanding my internal frustration. I used to rent cars from a company that got on my nerves. When I get off a plane, I normally don't feel like making small talk. The staff at the company I used to rent cars from had a policy of chitchatting with their customers. They even used a script. First they asked whether I was in town for business or pleasure, then they asked about the weather where I came from. On and on it went. I heard this script so many times I started having fun beating them to their own talking points. I'd often jump ahead on their script and ask the clerk, "Are you going to be able to have a little downtime while you're in town?" They'd just stare blankly at me because I'd hijacked their line.

One day, though, I was watching television and a commercial came on for National Car Rental. The commercial showed a guy walking through the rental office without talking to anybody. The character talked about how he hated having to make conversation with salespeople and how he loved walking straight to his car. I immediately changed rental car companies and have been happy ever since.

Speaking of car companies, CarMax is a chain of used car dealerships that aims most of their marketing collateral at the internal problem a customer experiences when looking for a used car—namely, the fear and frustration of having to interact with a used car salesman.

If you've ever walked onto a used car lot, you know the feeling. It's as though you're about to wear yourself out in an altercation with a professional wrestler.

Knowing their customers don't want to haggle over prices with a wannabe con artist, CarMax's business strategy is aimed at alleviating your fear of being lied to, cheated, or worked over in your car-buying experience. To do this, they have an agreement plan with their customers that ensures the price on the car is the price you'll pay, and lets you know their salespeople aren't compensated on a variable commission. They also highlight their quality certification and inspection process that ensures every car they sell is reliable.[2]

The external problem CarMax resolves is the need for a car, of course, but they hardly advertise about cars at all. Instead, their smart marketing department has focused on their customers' internal problems and, in doing so, entered one of the least-trusted industries in America and created a $15 billion phenomenon.[3]

Likewise, Starbucks exploded not just by offering customers a cup of coffee but by giving them a comfortable, sophisticated environment in which to relax and connect. When they walked into a Starbucks, customers felt good about themselves. Americans went from hanging out in diners and bars to lounging in a local, Italian-style coffee shop. By solving their customers' internal problems, Starbucks brought an entire industry to America. Thousands of European-style boutique coffee shops have popped up in nearly every small town in America, following Starbucks' lead.

In understanding how their customers wanted to feel, Starbucks took a product that Americans were used to paying fifty cents for (or drinking for almost free at home or at work) and were able to charge four or five dollars per cup. Starbucks customers are willing to pay more for their coffee because they sense greater value with each cup.

Understanding and talking about our customers' internal problems does more than create better advertising. Framing our products as a resolution to both external and internal problems increases the perceived value (and, I would argue, actual value) of those products. In other words, when you solve somebody's internal problem, you can charge more for your products.

Later, I'll guide you through a brainstorming exercise helping you identify some of your customers' internal problems, but before that, let's look at a third kind of problem our customers experience. This third level can help the story you are inviting customers into go from interesting to downright passion-inducing. Adding a philosophical problem is one of the main reasons a film will win Best Picture at the Academy Awards, and it will have your audience sitting on the edge of their seats. A good philosophical problem can help you turn disinterested customers into brand fanatics.

PHILOSOPHICAL PROBLEMS

Adding a philosophical problem creates depth and meaning in a story and is often the reason stories resonate and become fan favorites. The philosophical problem helps those who engage the story understand why the story matters in the overall epic narrative of humanity itself.

Why is it important that Tommy Boy should save his dad's company? I'll tell you why, because the people trying to take Tommy Boy down are lying thieves. This is a comedic story about honesty, family, integrity, and hard work versus deception, greed, and trickery.

Why is it important that Hamlet should avenge his father's death? Because his uncle is getting away with murder.

Why is it important that Bridget Jones should find love? Because the beauty and worth of every person deserves to be recognized and cherished by another.

A philosophical problem can best be talked about using terms like *ought* and *shouldn't*. For example: "Bad people shouldn't be allowed to win" and "People ought to be treated fairly."

In the movie *The King's Speech,* the external problem is presented in the form of King George's stutter. This external problem manifests the internal problem of the king's self-doubt and his own feeling that the wrong man now wears the crown. King George simply doesn't believe he has what it takes to lead his country. Philosophically, though, the stakes are much greater. Because the king must unify his people against the Nazis, the story takes on the philosophical problem of good versus evil.

What's the Deeper Meaning?

The reason people resonate so strongly with the philosophical problem in a story is because human beings want to be involved in a story that is larger than themselves. When a story represents (or speaks to) a cause, it expands beyond the screen or the page and stirs people to champion a cause, which gives the story itself considerably more import. Likewise, brands that give customers a voice in a larger narrative add value to their products by offering a deeper sense of meaning in their own story.

After creating their BrandScript, a global consulting firm my team worked with began to talk about how everybody deserved to work for a great manager. A pet store owner who came to us hung a sign in her window that said, "Pets deserve to eat healthy food too." A fun-loving travel agent came to us and adopted the seasonal line "Because this summer should be remembered forever."

Before music went digital, Tower Records promoted their stores by using the tagline "No Music, No Life." Not only did the tagline help them sell more than a billion dollars in records each year, but they sold thousands of bumper stickers and T-shirts featuring the tagline to fans who wanted to associate with the philosophical belief that music mattered.

Is there a deeper story your brand contributes to? Can your products be positioned as tools your customers use to fight back against something that ought not to be? If so, let's include some philosophical stakes in our messaging.

The Perfect Brand Promise

If we really want to satisfy our customers and create brand evangelists, we can offer much more than products or services; we can offer to resolve an external, internal, and philosophical problem whenever they engage our business.

Storytellers use this formula to endear and satisfy audiences all the time. The strategy is to resolve the hero's external, internal, and philosophical problem in a single, well-crafted scene. At the end of the blockbuster movie *Star Wars: A New Hope*, when Luke Skywalker shoots a photon torpedo through the exhaust portal in an empire-constructed planetary ship called the Death Star, Luke resolves the external problem of destroying the Death Star, the internal problem of self-doubt he felt about being a Jedi, and the philosophical problem of good versus evil. When all three levels of conflict were resolved at once, the audience felt three levels of relief, and the movie itself became a phenomenon that generated countless sequels and spin-offs and an entire new world at Disney's Hollywood Studios.

The climactic scene is often called the "obligatory" scene because by opening the external, internal, and philosophical story gap early in the movie, the storyteller is obligated to close all three levels of conflict at the story's end. This idea is important for those of us who are building a brand. Our products, if we want them to succeed in the marketplace, should offer to solve a problem, soothe a feeling, and, if possible, contribute to some sort of justice-oriented agenda. Then, upon purchase, our solutions need to fulfill all three promises. If we can accomplish this (and use clear words to explain how we did), we can expect customers to fall in love with our products and our brand.

If we really want our business to grow, we should position

our products as the resolution to an external, internal, and philosophical problem and frame the "Buy Now" button as the action a customer must take to close the story gap we've opened in their minds.

Let's look at how some familiar brands have positioned their products as the solution to external, internal, and philosophical problems:

TESLA MOTOR CARS:

Villain: Gas-guzzling, inferior technology

External: I need a better car.

Internal: I want to be an early adopter of new technology.

Philosophical: My choice of car ought to help save the environment and perform better at the same time.

NESPRESSO HOME COFFEE MACHINES:

Villain: Coffee machines that make bad coffee

External: I want better-tasting coffee at home.

Internal: I want my home coffee machine to make me feel sophisticated.

Philosophical: I shouldn't have to be a barista to make gourmet coffee at home.

EDWARD JONES FINANCIAL PLANNING:

Villain: Financial firms that don't listen to their customers

External: I need investment help.

Internal: I'm confused about how to do this (especially with all the tech-driven resources out there).

Philosophical: If I'm going to invest my money, I deserve an adviser who will thoughtfully explain financial complexities to me in person.

WHAT CHALLENGES ARE YOU HELPING YOUR CUSTOMER OVERCOME?

Identifying a villain that is causing an external, internal, and philosophical problem may seem daunting, but it will come to you if you commit to working it out in a brainstorming session. But be careful to keep it simple. Many of our clients want to include three villains, seven external problems, four internal problems, and so on. But, as I've already mentioned, stories are best when they are clear. If we are going to create memorable sound bites, we'll need to make choices.

Is there a single villain your brand stands against? What external problem is that villain causing? How is that external problem making your customers feel? And why is it unjust for people to have to suffer at the hands of this villain?

These are the four questions we want to answer in the problem section of our StoryBrand BrandScript. When we do, the story our brand is telling will take shape because our hero, the customer who wants something, is being challenged. Will they win? Will their problems be resolved?

Perhaps. The thing is, they will have to engage your brand to find out.

CLARIFY YOUR MESSAGE SO CUSTOMERS LISTEN

- Go to StoryBrand.AI and either create a BrandScript or log in to your existing BrandScript.
- Either alone or with your team, brainstorm all of the literal and metaphorical villains your brand takes a stand against.
- Brainstorm the external problems your brand resolves. Is there one that seems to represent the widest swath of products?
- Brainstorm the internal problem (frustration or doubt) your customers are feeling as it relates to your brand. Is there one that stands out as a universal experience for your customers?
- Is your brand part of a larger, more important story? Is there a philosophical wrong your brand stands against?
- Once you finish your brainstorming session, make the four StoryBrand BrandScript decisions that will allow you to create sound bites for the second element of your StoryBrand BrandScript.

Has a Problem

Villain

____

____

External

____

____

Internal

____

____

Philosophical

____

____

CHAPTER 6

AND MEETS A GUIDE

StoryBrand Principle Three: Customers aren't looking for another hero; they're looking for a guide.

Shakespeare was right—a person's life is made up of many acts. As a book writer, though, I prefer to see these acts as chapters. If you look back on your life, you'll likely see them too. There is the chapter when you grew up poor and the chapter when you began to understand you could dream big and the chapter about the importance of family and relationships and the chapter in which you realize that giving is more fulfilling than getting and so on and so on. There is an evolution to our maturity, and when you look back, it's a beautiful evolution. I believe one of the main miracles of life is the fact that we get to transform.

No two lives are the same, yet we share common chapters. Every human being is on a transformational journey.

It's easy to recognize these chapters by their events, or what writer and story scholar James Scott Bell calls "doorways of no return."[1] This might have been our parents' divorce, our first crush, a rejection from somebody we loved, or having absolutely nailed the moonwalk when the crowd gathered around us at the junior high dance.

In stories, events mark the beginnings and endings of our chapters. But if we look closer, we will see something else or, more accurately, somebody else.

The events that define our chapters are often instigated or interpreted by mystical characters who help us along the way. Story scholars call these characters by many names, such as wizards or mentors or helpers. I choose to call these mystical characters *guides*—those who step into our lives and help us face our challenges so that we can overcome them and transform into better versions of ourselves.

In his book *The Seven Basic Plots*, Christopher Booker describes how a guide is introduced into the story this way:

> A hero or heroine falls under a dark spell which eventually traps them in some wintry state, akin to a living death: physical or spiritual imprisonment, sleep, sickness or some other form of enchantment. For a long time they languish in this frozen condition. Then a miraculous act of redemption takes place, focused on a particular figure who helps to liberate the hero or heroine from imprisonment. From the depths of darkness they are brought up into glorious light.[2]

EVERY HERO IS LOOKING FOR A GUIDE

Our first guides came to us early. I'm talking about our mother and father, who loved us more than they loved themselves, who sacrificed for us and taught us the ways of the world. They taught us language and belonging and connection and our first words and letters and numbers. They read us stories about characters who faced troubles but showed courage. Later, many of our teachers and coaches played the role of guide by helping us understand the importance of working hard, and they taught us to believe we could accomplish more than we previously thought possible. For many of us, guides have included poets we've read, leaders who gave us a voice in the halls of power, therapists who helped us make sense of and solve our challenges, and yes, even brands that offered encouragement and tools that helped us overcome our challenges.

Guides are important in stories because they are important in life. Every human being knows that the wisdom it takes to navigate life is passed down, that no human can figure it out on their own. If a hero solves her own problem in a story, the audience will find it difficult to suspend disbelief. Why? Because we intuitively know if she could solve her own problem, she wouldn't have gotten into trouble in the first place. Storytellers use the guide character, then, to encourage the hero and equip them to win the day.

You've seen the guide in nearly every story you've read, listened to, or watched: Frodo is helped by Gandalf, Katniss is guided by Haymitch, and Luke Skywalker is shown the way of a Jedi by the all-knowing Yoda. Hamlet was guided by his father's ghost, just as Romeo was taught the ways of love by Juliet.

Human beings wake up every morning self-identifying as the hero of their own story. They are troubled by external, internal, and philosophical conflicts, and they know they can't solve these problems on their own. For this reason, all human beings are seeking guides. Certainly we are inspired by stories of other heroes overcoming great challenges, but what we really need when the conflict is rising in our own lives is not another hero—what we need is a guide.

The fatal mistake many brands make, especially young brands who believe they have something to prove, is positioning themselves as the hero in the story rather than the guide. As I've already mentioned, a brand that positions itself as the hero is destined to lose.

The Fatal Mistake

The ramifications of positioning our brand as the hero could be fatal. Consider the launch of the music streaming service Tidal. Never heard of it? There's a reason you likely haven't. Rapper Jay-Z founded the company with a personal investment of a whopping $56 million and a mission to "get everyone to respect music again."[3] Instead of being owned by music studios or tech companies, Tidal would be owned by musicians, allowing them to cut out the middleman and take their products directly to market. As a result, artists would be able to pocket more of the profits.

It may sound like a good business idea (and it was), but Jay-Z failed to consider the mistake of positioning himself and other artists as the heroes. He rightly saw an injustice in the world of music—namely, that artists were not getting paid for their own work. Instead, the money was going to record labels. But in publicly positioning artists as the heroes fighting for a cause, he forgot that the artists weren't the customers, the music-loving public was the customer. After all, were only artists going to buy music from each other? No. Under the StoryBrand framework, the customer must always be the hero and the brand must always play the guide.

In the months leading up to the launch of Tidal, Jay-Z recruited sixteen well-known musicians who agreed to release exclusive content on his platform in exchange for a percentage of equity. In their multimillion-dollar rollout, the artists stood shoulder to shoulder at a press conference to explain their mission. Predictably, this is where everything fell apart.

If only Jay-Z, in other ways a genius, had understood the age-old rules of story, he might have avoided walking into a minefield.

"Water is free," Jay-Z quipped. "Music is $6 but no one wants to pay for music." He continued, somewhat confusingly, "You should drink free water from the tap—it's a beautiful thing. And if you want to hear the most beautiful song, then support the artist."[4]

Social media, especially Twitter (now X), eviscerated Jay-Z and Tidal. Thousands reminded him to check with the people who paid his bills to discover water wasn't actually free. Overnight, an artist who built his career speaking for the people sounded entitled. The public became nauseated listening to a row of famous multimillionaire musicians guilt-trip them into paying more for their music. The crucial mistake: Jay-Z failed to answer the one question lingering in the subconscious of every hero customer: *How are you helping me win the day?* Tidal existed to help the artists win the day, not customers. And so it failed to launch successfully. The real tragedy of Tidal is that both the product and the cause (an artist's right to be paid for their work) are just causes. I actually subscribe to Tidal myself, not because I champion the rights of artists but because the streaming service contains larger downloads that make the music sound much, much better. How should Jay-Z have positioned Tidal? In my view, he should have positioned the existing streaming services as the villains because they are shrinking the sound the artists had created and shorting music lovers of the best possible experience. The artists could have talked endlessly about how they make music for the fans and that by streaming through Tidal, fans could finally hear music the way it was meant to be heard, the way the artist intended. The controlling idea behind the campaign could have been "Music the way it was mean to be heard" and could have been repeated in all forms of messaging and marketing, thus helping word spread about what makes Tidal different.

In short, any message that can be framed as a contribution to a "power to the people" movement will trump any message that is framed as a "power to the powerful" money grab. Of course, a "power to the powerful" money grab was likely never in the mind of Jay-Z, yet we should all be careful about how our positioning is perceived by our hero customers. If our fans don't believe we are fully doing business for them, they will move on to another brand.

In fact, I had no interest in Tidal when I heard what the artists were doing to protect their own paychecks, but I signed up immediately when I found out you could listen to music online that rivaled the sound quality of vinyl. In other words, when I realized that Tidal was actually helping me, the hero customer, win the day, I bought the product.

Jay-Z sold his majority interest in Tidal for $350 million, so he definitely didn't lose. However, the streaming service should have sold for billions of dollars. There's a lesson in the Tidal story for all of us: Positioning yourself as the hero devalues your offering. In fact, it would be a great private equity play to shop for brands with terrific products but mistakenly positioning themselves as heroes in the story. Anybody hunting for a business to buy could seek out businesses making the "hero mistake," buy them cheap, change the messaging (and culture of the company) to position the brand as the guide, and then see a predictable increase in both revenue and the overall value of the business itself.

Position your customer as the hero and your brand as the guide. If you don't, your brand will struggle to survive. The hero is *always* the person pulling out their wallet to make a purchase. The hero is *never* the people who make the product. If you remember that, you are more likely to get your messaging (and your business strategy) right.

The larger point here is simple: the day we stop losing sleep over our problems and start losing sleep over our customers' problems is the day our business will transform into a brand customers love.

Positioning Yourself as the Hero Makes You Look Weak

Why should we never position ourselves as the hero? Because in stories, heroes are weak. If we are tempted to position our brand as the hero because heroes are strong and capable and the center of attention, we should think again about the nature of a hero. In stories, the hero is never the strongest character. Heroes are often ill-equipped and filled with self-doubt. They aren't sure of themselves and they wonder if they have what it takes to get the job done. They are often reluctant to take action, having been thrown into the story rather than willingly engaging their challenges. In fact, it is my view that in a good story the hero should be the second-weakest character after the victim. The guide, however, is strong. The guide has already "been there and done that" and has conquered the hero's challenge in their own backstory. Haymitch had already won the Hunger Games. Yoda had already transformed into a Jedi. They may have been weak at one time, but the guide now has the very characteristics and abilities the hero must attain to win the day.

The guide is the character in the story who has the strength and the authority to help the hero win. Still, the story is not really about the guide despite the important role they play. The story must always be focused on the hero, and if a storyteller (or business leader) forgets this, the audience will get confused about who the story is really about and will lose interest. In fact, my wife and I went to see a movie in the theaters last year and were slightly disappointed as the credits rolled. We felt a slight cognitive dissonance that comes when a screenwriter didn't quite get it right. What was wrong with the script? The guide transformed. By that I mean there was a hero who was up against a significant challenge, and instead of the guide only serving the hero's story, the screenwriter thought it would give a greater sense of depth if the guide also experienced a little of their own transformation, a little unknowing, a little self-doubt. The treatment backfired. Why? Because the audience couldn't figure out who the hero was and who the guide was. The guide *must* be strong and all-knowing. The guide must be confident, that way the spotlight is fully on the hero and their transformation. If both the hero and the guide are transforming in a story, who the heck is the story about?

This idea that the guide must be strong and competent is best demonstrated in Walt Disney's perennial hit movie *Mary Poppins*. In the timeless adaptation of P. L. Travers's eight-book series of the same name, Mary Poppins is the guide. The father, George Banks, is actually the hero of the story, transforming from an uncaring, distracted, hard-nosed father into a soft, caring, and attentive dad in the end. Mary Poppins, however, guides the entire family into an empathetic reminder of the magic of childhood, shaping the children and the father to be engaged, compassionate, moral, and well-behaved. She does this with lessons of wisdom and perspective, all from a place of ultimate authority. In fact, in an early scene in the movie Mary Poppins uses a measuring tape to gauge the yawning chasm between the children's need for development and her own authority as the guide. As she lifts the measuring tape to the height of the children, the tape reveals the children as "extremely stubborn and suspicious" and "rather inclined to giggle and doesn't put things away," respectively. When Mary Poppins measures herself, however, the magical tape declares her "practically perfect in every way."

In a confrontational scene near the end of the film, the hero, George Banks, confronts Mary Poppins, demanding that she explain herself and her actions. She stands looking down at the confused hero from the top of the stairs and exclaims that Mary Poppins does not explain herself to anybody.

In the overall story of life, there are guides and there are heroes. I'm certainly not suggesting that you, as a brand, never offer to explain yourself; however, we should learn a thing or two from Mary Poppins: As guides, it is paramount we be competent and strong. The hero is counting on us to know more than they know and to have a solution to their greatest problem. The guide, then, must live in service of the hero, and if the guide is not competent, they are useless. Can you imagine a candidate running for president exclaiming, "I have always wanted to be president but I've never really believed in myself, nor do I know what I am doing, but if you vote for me I will try my hardest to figure it out." This candidate would generate a great deal of interest and differentiate themselves from the rest of the field but ultimately would gain very few votes. When we look for a leader, we enjoy a backstory of transformation but a current demonstration of competency.

That said, arrogance never serves anybody and is ultimately a sign of defensiveness and weakness. Mary Poppins is sure of her philosophy, sure of her plan, and sure of her mission—to transform the family into a healthy and functioning unit led by a patriarch who is engaged and compassionate—but she is not in the story to serve herself or her own transformation. She is in the story to serve the family. The problem in the Banks family was always the father, and by the end of the story, the problem is solved.

The idea that the guide must serve the hero is true in business, in politics, and even in your own family. People are looking for a guide to help them, not another hero.

Those who realize the epic story of life is not about them but actually about the people around them somehow win in the end. It's counterintuitive, but it's true. In fact, leaders who think the story of life is all about them may achieve temporary successes but are usually remembered in history's narrative as villains. If you make the story about you, you will lose.

THE TWO CHARACTERISTICS OF A GUIDE

At StoryBrand, we have seen thousands of businesses experience an increase in customer engagement once they stopped positioning themselves as the hero and started positioning themselves as the guide. After filtering their message through the StoryBrand framework, thousands of business leaders have realized their websites, email blasts, digital ads, television commercials, and even their elevator pitches have been broadcasting a self-sabotaging message. However, adjusting our focus so that it is clearly on the customer and playing the guide by offering that customer a solution to their problem will radically change the way we talk about, and even do, business.

So what do we have to do to be recognized as the guide in our customers' lives?

We must demonstrate two characteristics in order to be recognized as a guide: empathy and competency.

When Luke Skywalker meets Yoda, he encounters the perfect guide. Luke is ill-equipped for the task before him, and Yoda is the endearing character who empathetically understands Luke's dilemma. This empathy would be of little service, of course, were it not for Yoda's competency as a Jedi himself. Yoda understands Luke's dilemma and has mastered the skills he must now develop if he is going to win the day.

The guide must have this precise one-two punch of empathy and competency in order to move the hero and the story along. These are the characteristics the hero is looking for, and when he or she senses them, they know they have found their guide.

The Incredible Power of Empathy

When Bill Clinton delivered his now-famous line "I feel your pain" in 1992, he did more than just clinch a victory over George H. W. Bush in a close presidential election; he positioned himself as the guide in the American voters' story. In fact, many pundits believe Clinton locked up the election during a town hall debate in which Bush gave a rambling answer to a young woman when she asked what the national debt meant to the average American. Clinton countered Bush's linear, cerebral answer by asking the woman if she knew anybody who'd lost their job. He asked whether it pained her that she had friends out of work, and when the woman said yes, he went on to explain how the national debt is tied to the well-being of every American, even her and her friends.[5] That's empathy. What did the audience sense? They sensed competency in Bush but empathy and competency in Clinton. Did Bush care? Of course, but unless we use sound bites to express our care, our audience does not connect. As a mentor of mine once told me: don't put people in the mind-reading business.

When we empathize with our customers' dilemma, we create a bond of trust. People trust those who understand them, and they trust brands that understand them too.

Oprah Winfrey, an undeniably successful guide to millions, once explained that the three things every human being wants most are to be seen, heard, and understood. This is the essence of empathy.

Empathetic statements start with words like, "We understand how it feels to . . ." or "Nobody should have to experience . . ." or "Like you, we are frustrated by . . ." or, in the case of one commercial inviting Toyota owners to engage their local Toyota service center, simply, "We care about your Toyota."

Expressing empathy isn't difficult. Once we've identified our customers' internal problems, we simply need to let them know we understand and would like to help them find a resolution. Scan your marketing material and make sure you've told your customers that you care. Again, customers won't know you care until you tell them.

ARE YOU LIKE ME?

Empathy is more than just sentimental slogans though. Real empathy means letting customers know we care about them in the same way we care about ourselves. Customers look for brands they have something in common with. Remember, the human brain likes to conserve calories, so when a customer realizes they have a lot in common with a brand, they fill in all their cognitive dissonance with trust. Essentially, when we highlight the aspects of ourselves or our brand that we have in common with our customer, the customer batches their thinking, meaning they think in "chunks" rather than details. Here's what I mean by "thinking in chunks." Last night, my wife and I attended a dinner party and sat next to a couple we'd not met before. As we started talking, I noticed how instinctively human beings search for commonality. When my wife discovered that the couple had grown up in Louisiana, there was an instant connection as she herself hails from the north shore of Lake Pontchartrain. As humans get to know each other, they search for shared places and people and experiences, thus increasing the feeling that there is a mutual understanding of life and giving us the feeling that the person we are talking to is safe. That is why finding and expressing commonality—whether taste in music or shared values or shared stages of life—and talking about those commonalities is such a powerful marketing tool.

Once, while counseling a politician, I explained that even if you are in a room of people who are completely different than you, you must find and focus on a common experience, especially if you need to express disagreement. For example: *Like you, I am deeply concerned about the cost of health care, but I'm equally concerned about government incompetency to run our health-care system. In my view, socialized medicine disincentivizes innovation, which could ultimately lead to a radical decline in patient care and even longevity of life. You and I are the same in that we believe Americans are paying too much for too little when it comes to health care, but if we put our heads together, practical people like us will find a solution. You're right, though, that this problem must be dealt with. We certainly agree on that.*

The point is this: Your brand and your customer are alike. You have shared experiences and a shared view of life. A recent Discover Card television campaign tapped into the power of empathy by showing customers who call Discover's customer service line and end up talking to an exact replica of themselves. As they talk, the customer realizes they have everything in common with their credit card company; in fact, they are exactly the same. The message? Discover Card will take care of you the same way you would take care of yourself. We understand you. We know you.

The Necessity of Competency

In the first edition of *Building a StoryBrand* I listed the two characteristics of a guide as empathy and authority, but the word *authority* never sat right with me. After all, nobody likes a know-it-all and nobody wants to be preached at. The better word, then, is *competency.* As a guide, you do not have to be perfect, but you do have to be competent in your field of expertise. This is paramount. This is why Mary Poppins refused to budge in her self-confidence as a guide. Were she to have compromised her higher ground as it related to her competency to positively shape the future of a child, the movie would have had two heroes and no guide and as such would have been ruined. Competency matters, and if you actually have it, let's not mess around with self-deprecation. Your hero needs more than a friend; they need a useful friend.

Imagine walking into a nutritionist's office for the first time, determined to get into the best shape of your life.

"I'd like to lose thirty pounds," you might tell her. "It's been a struggle for a long time, but I'm ready."

How would you feel if the nutritionist, upon hearing your stated objective, looked at you, sighed, pinched an inch of the spare tire around their waist, and said, "Me too."

It wouldn't take you long to realize you'd chosen the wrong nutritionist.

The guide needs to know what they are doing and should have serious experience helping other heroes win the day. Wouldn't you agree that Gordon Ramsey's television show would be ruined if, instead of being the authoritative chef and restaurateur, he shyly confessed he knew nothing about fixing a restaurant but looked forward to learning *with* his hopeless client?

At this point in the journey, many readers wonder how they can demonstrate their own competency without making themselves the hero. It's a good question. The truth is, as a guide, you can talk about yourself all day long. To play the guide doesn't mean that you go quiet and humble. In fact, you'll notice that Mary Poppins gets much more screen time than George Banks, even though the story is largely about his transformation. The key to playing the guide, though, is to tell only the parts of your story that support your care for the customer and your competency to help them.

As customers view our websites, commercials, or emails, they simply want to check off a box in the back of their minds that gives them confidence in our ability to help them. And our backstory can help. I recently had dinner with Mary and Madison Lee, who run a skin care line called Nēmah. The origin story of Nēmah serves as a great example of a brand telling the part of its story that positions the brand as the guide. In short, Mary had trouble finding a skin care line she could trust during the pregnancy of her first child. It turns out many skin care products are not safe for the mother and are especially harmful for the development of a child. She and her husband then created Nēmah's line of products using only ingredients that are safe and healthy so that mothers would have a brand they could trust. By tapping into a serious concern mothers everywhere have in common and telling their own story about that concern (empathy) along with the science they discovered in their research (competency), they have built a phenomenally successful brand positioning themselves as former struggling heroes turned empathetic and competent guides who are helping other heroes win the day.

There are five easy ways to add evidence of competency to your marketing and messaging.

1. **Testimonials:** Let others do the talking for you. If you have satisfied customers, place a few testimonials on your website. Testimonials give potential customers the gift of going second. They know others just like them who have bought your products and experienced success. You don't need many testimonials as long as they are short and speak directly to how *your* product solved *their* problem. Three is a great number to start with and will serve the need of ensuring that most customers know that you know what you are doing. Also, avoid rambling testimonials that heap endless praise on your brand. It won't take long for a customer to trust you, so keep a testimonial brief. If it looks too long, they won't read it. Most customers scan websites. The shorter the sound bites, the more they will engage and retain.
2. **Statistics:** How many satisfied customers have you helped? How much money have you helped them save? A simple statement like the email marketing platform Keap's "125,000 users trust [our] award-winning automation software"[6] is all your potential customer needs. Numeric evidence scratches the itch of the left-brained consumer who loves numbers, statistics, and facts.
3. **Awards:** If you've won a few awards for your work, feel free to include small logos or indications of those awards at the bottom of your page. These are hardly necessary, but if you've got them, flaunt them a little. Awards go a long way in earning your customer's trust, even if they've never heard of the award.
4. **Press Mentions:** If you've been featured in the press, simply state "Featured by" and the logo of the press that

has featured you. You can also list endorsements from either press or influencers as a way of creating social proof that demonstrates your competency.

5. **Logos:** If you provide a business-to-business product or service, place logos of known businesses you've worked with in your marketing collateral. Customers want to know you've helped other businesses overcome their same challenges. When your customer recognizes another business you've worked with, it provides social proof you have the ability to help them win the day.

Take a minute to scan your marketing material and ask yourself whether you've provided evidence of competency. Remember, you don't have to brag about yourself. Testimonials, logos, awards, press mentions, and statistics will allow customers to check the "trust" box in the back of their minds as it relates to your products or services. Your customers are asking themselves questions like, "Does this brand know what they're doing? Is investing my time and money going to be worth it? Can they really help me solve my problem?"

HOW TO MAKE A GREAT FIRST IMPRESSION

When people meet your brand, it's as though they are meeting a person. They're wondering if the two of you will get along, whether you can help them live a better life, whether they want to associate their identity with your brand, and ultimately, whether they can trust you.

Harvard Business professor Amy Cuddy has spent more than fifteen years studying how business leaders can make a positive first impression. Cuddy distilled her research into two questions people subconsciously ask when meeting someone new: "Can I trust this person?" and "Can I respect this person?" In her book *Presence*, Cuddy explains that human beings value trust so highly, it's only after trust is established that a person begins to consider getting to know us further.[7]

When we express empathy, we help our customers answer Cuddy's first question, "Can I trust this person?"

Providing evidence of competency helps our customers answer the second question, "Can I respect this person?"

The same two characteristics that help us make a great first impression with people at a cocktail party also work to help our brand make a great first impression with potential customers.

Once we express empathy and demonstrate competence, we can position our brand as the guide our customer has been looking for. This will make a significant difference in the way they remember us, understand us, and ultimately become willing to engage with our products and services.

That said, even though our customers like us and trust us, it doesn't mean they're going to place an order. There is still a yawning chasm between a customer's trust and their decision to invest their hard-earned money in what we're offering. What are they looking for next? We'll talk about an important aspect in the buying journey in the next chapter.

For now, though, brainstorm how you can position yourself as the guide in your customer's life by expressing empathy and providing evidence of competency.

CLARIFY YOUR MESSAGE SO CUSTOMERS LISTEN

- Go to StoryBrand.AI and either create a BrandScript or log in to your existing BrandScript.
- Either alone or with a team, brainstorm empathetic statements you can make so your customers know you care about their internal problem.
- Brainstorm the many ways you can demonstrate competency by exploring potential testimonials, statistics that demonstrate competence, awards you've won, press mentions, or logos from other businesses you've helped.
- Once you finish your brainstorming session, make the two StoryBrand BrandScript decisions that will allow you to fill out section 3.

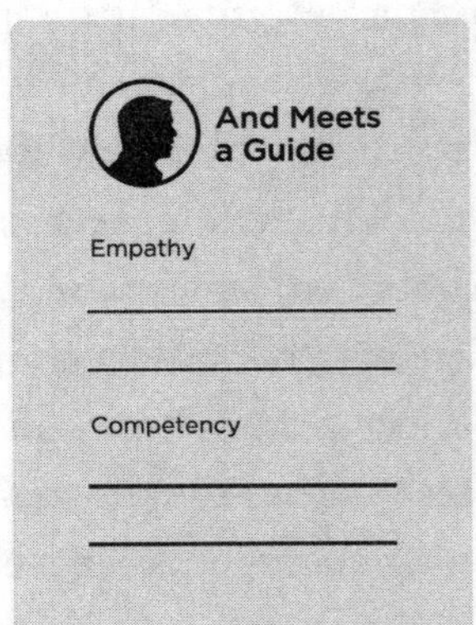

CHAPTER 7

WHO GIVES THEM A PLAN

StoryBrand Principle Four: Customers trust a guide who gives them a plan in the form of baby steps.

At this point in our customer's journey, we've identified something they want, which got the story started. Then we proved we understood their deepest challenges and pain points, which further opened a story gap and drew them to our brand. Then we introduced ourselves as the guide by expressing empathy and providing evidence of competency, which helped establish trust. Yet even with all this, the customer isn't likely to place an order. Some customers will go ahead at this point and place an order, but a percentage are wanting more.

If we've positioned ourselves as the guide, our customers likely want to know more and are feeling hopeful that we can help them. But feeling hopeful about our ability to help them and jumping into a commitment by pulling out their pocketbooks are two different things. When a customer places an order, they're essentially saying, "I believe you can help me solve my problem, and I believe it so much I'm willing to put skin in the game. I'm willing to part with my hard-earned dollars."

Commitments are tricky for our customers because as soon as they make a commitment, they run the risk of losing their money. But more than their money, their time and their identity as a person who makes smart buying decisions are also at risk. Most customers are not going to take that chance just yet.

When a customer is deciding whether to buy something, we should picture them standing on the edge of a large, rushing creek. It's true they want what's on the other side of the creek, but as they stand there, they hear a waterfall downstream. What happens if they fall into the creek? What would life look like if they went over those falls? These are the kinds of subconscious questions our customers ponder as they hover their little arrow over the "Buy Now" button. *What if it doesn't work? What if I'm a fool for buying this? How long will it take to work? What if I buy it and never use it?*

Your customer is also asking another question: How do I get from where I am to the place where I've adopted this new product in my life? After all, your customer's life, as unstable as it is, is familiar. And change is hard. So installing a new software or changing toothpaste or living with a new schedule or driving somewhere they've never been or changing banks or breakfast routines or vitamin supplements presents a kind of mystery about how life will be different, and that just seems like something they are going to want to deal with tomorrow.

For years I wanted a new wearable fitness tracker called a Whoop, and I mean for years. My friends had all raved about it and I knew it would help me, but I had this subconscious cognitive dissonance about whether I had to plug it in all the time or download a smart phone application or enter my credit card or wear it to bed. So I just put it off. It wasn't until I went to their website and saw a simple three-step instruction on how to get started that I bought the thing. Honestly, it took me all of three minutes to set it up and start using it. To think I went years without buying it because, well, adopting a new habit created a slight amount of cognitive dissonance I just didn't want to deal with. That story may sound silly, but I assure you there are thousands of people who "feel" cognitive dissonance about your products or services, and if you don't give them a few simple steps they can take to easily cross from unknowing into knowing, they are less likely to spend money with you.

Cognitive dissonance shows up in your customers' behavior as indecisiveness and indifference. Essentially, your customer is thinking, *I've got this problem I need to solve but I can probably live with it a little longer, so maybe I will just deal with finding the solution tomorrow or the next day*. Metaphorically, your customer is stuck on the wrong side of the creek, but the shore is dry, so why figure out how to cross the creek at all? In order to ease our customers' concerns and relieve their cognitive dissonance, we need to place large stones in that rushing creek. When we identify a few baby steps our customers can take to get across the creek, we remove much of the perceived risk and increase their comfort level about placing an order. It's as though we're saying, "First, step here. See, it's easy. Then step here, then here, and then you'll be on the other side, and your problem will be resolved."

In the StoryBrand framework, we refer to these baby steps as a *plan*.

Once, while consulting for a national mattress brand, I asked their sales representatives to give the customer a three-step plan just before asking for the order. Instead of saying, "Can I write this mattress up for you?" the retail sales representative said, "The process of buying a mattress from us works in three steps: you choose a mattress; then we deliver it; then, if you want, we remove your old mattress so you don't have to worry about how you will dispose of it. This mattress seems to be the one that is perfect for you. Would you like to make a purchase?" Not to my surprise, when the mattress representatives inserted a simple three-step plan in the sales process, sales went up. Why? Because cognitive dissonance was removed before the sales rep asked for the money.

Whenever a customer says, "Let me think about it" or "Let me get back to you," what they are really saying is that they've got some cognitive dissonance and could use some space before making a buying decision. Of course, nobody goes home with them to answer questions and relieve the cognitive dissonance, so the customer never places an order. To be sure, I don't think the customer is trying to get out of placing an order; I think they actually want to place an order, but as long as they feel that cognitive dissonance, they aren't going to. Therefore, we've got to relieve that cognitive dissonance right there in the conversation, or in the email, or on the website, or even in the product sales copy.

Even in stories, the guide often gives the hero a plan. In the movie *Moneyball*, for example, Peter Brand (the guide) gives Billy Beane (the hero) a plan he can employ to turn his baseball team around. In a series of steps, Billy will begin using an algorithm to choose players rather than relying on anecdotal evidence from his antiquated coaching staff. In the new way of running a baseball team, Billy is going to begin to trust the numbers and run the team the way a hedge-fund manager might run his hedge fund. Step one: trust the numbers. Step two: turn the coaching culture around. Step three: win games.

In *Star Wars: A New Hope*, Luke Skywalker is told to fly his X-wing fighter into the trench on the Death Star, shoot a photon torpedo through an exhaust valve, and then get out of there before the Death Star blows up. In other words, he's given a three-step plan.

In nearly every movie you can think of, the guide gives the hero a plan. The plan is the bridge the hero must cross in order to arrive at the climactic scene. Rocky has to train using nontraditional methods, Tommy Boy has to embark on a national sales trip, and Juliet must drink the potion the apothecary gives her in order to trick her family into thinking she's died so she can be free to run away with Romeo.

A plan serves the narrative by narrowing the focus of the plot. It also, quite pragmatically, gives the hero something to do that kills twenty minutes in the second half of act 2.

THE PLAN ENCOURAGES THE CUSTOMER TO MOVE FORWARD

In business, the plan can take many forms, but all effective plans do two things: they clarify what doing business with us will look like and they remove the sense of risk a customer might feel before committing to our product or service.

Remember the mantra "If you confuse, you lose"? Not having a plan is a guaranteed way to create cognitive dissonance.

After potential customers visit our website or listen to us give a keynote or read an email we've sent, they're all wondering the same thing: *What would my next step be if I wanted to move forward?* If we don't clearly guide them with next steps, the customer experiences a little bit of confusion, and because they can hear that waterfall downstream, they use that confusion as an excuse not to do business with us.

The fact we have communicated our offer clearly is not enough to motivate our customer at this point. If we're selling a storage system a customer can install in their garage, they hover over that "Buy Now" button, subconsciously wondering whether it will work for them, how hard it will be to install, and whether it will sit in boxes unopened like the last product they bought. But when we spell out how easy the storage system is to install and let them know they can get started in three easy steps, they are more likely to place an order.

Specifically, if you are selling garage shelves, you want to tell them to

1. measure their space,
2. order the items that fit, and
3. install it in minutes using basic tools.

Even though these steps may seem obvious to the people who made the product, the steps aren't obvious to the customer. Placing stones in the creek greatly increases the chance the customer will cross the creek.

THE PROCESS PLAN

At StoryBrand we've identified two plans you can use to effectively encourage customers to do business with you. The first kind of plan, and the one we recommend all our clients employ, is a process plan.

A process plan can describe the steps a customer needs to take to buy our product, or the steps they need to take to use our product after they buy it, or a mixture of both.

For instance, if you're selling an expensive, service-based product, you might break down the steps like this:

1. Schedule an appointment.
2. Allow us to create a customized plan.
3. Let's execute the plan together.

Whether we're selling a financial product, a medical procedure, a university education, or any other complicated solution, a process plan takes the confusion out of our customer's journey by breaking down the process into baby steps.

Another kind of process plan would be the post-purchase process plan. This plan is best used when our customers might have problems imagining how they would use our product after they buy it. For instance, with a complicated piece of software, we might want to spell out the steps or even the phases a customer would take after they make the purchase:

1. Download the software.
2. Integrate your database into the new system.
3. Revolutionize your customer interaction.

The post-purchase process plan does the same thing as a pre-purchase process plan in the sense that it alleviates confusion. When a customer is looking at the wide span between themselves and the integration of a complicated product, they're less likely to make a purchase. But when they read your plan, they think to themselves, *Oh, I can do that. That's not so hard*, and then they click "Buy Now."

A process plan can also combine the pre- and post-purchase steps. For instance:

1. Test-drive a car.
2. Purchase the car.
3. Enjoy free maintenance for life.

Again, the key to *any* plan's success is to alleviate confusion about next steps. What steps do they need to take to do business with you? Spell out those steps, and it'll be as though you've paved a sidewalk through a field. More people will cross the field.

We frequently get questions about how many steps a process plan should have. The answer varies, of course, but we recommend at least three and no more than six. If doing business with you requires more than six steps, break down those steps into phases and describe the phases. In reality, you might guide your customer through twenty or thirty steps, but studies show when you bombard customers with information, buying decreases.

Remember, the whole point of creating a plan is to alleviate customers' confusion. Having more than four steps may actually add to, rather than reduce, confusion. The key is to simplify their journey so they are more likely to do business with you.

THE AGREEMENT PLAN

If process plans are about alleviating confusion, agreement plans are about alleviating fears.

An agreement plan is best understood as a list of agreements you make with your customers to help them overcome their fear of doing business with you.

Earlier I talked about CarMax and how they resolve the customer's agitation of having to deal with a used car salesman. One of the tools they use to communicate that customers don't have to encounter this internal fear is an agreement plan. CarMax's four-point agreement plan includes the promise that customers will never have to haggle. Afraid you'll be stuck with a lemon? CarMax refuses to sell a car that doesn't meet their standards, and they put every car through a renewal process to be sure it earns their quality certification seal.[1]

Today, CarMax sells more cars than its next three competitors combined. In fact, not long ago, *Automotive News* named CarMax the undisputed used car champion.[2] As I mentioned in chapter 5, CarMax rarely advertises the solution to their customers' external problems (that is, the need for a used car). Instead, they focus on their customers' internal problem, the fear of interacting with a used car dealer, and they alleviate this fear with an agreement plan.

An agreement plan can also work to increase the perceived value of a service you promise to provide. For instance, Newt Gingrich's "Contract with America" is an example of an agreement plan. Newt was a relatively unknown congressman from Georgia who led a takeover in both houses of Congress by making an agreement with voters. Newt simply took age-old conservative talking points, turned them into a list, and said, "If you vote for us, we'll do all these things." More than three hundred conservative legislators signed on, and Newt became an overnight presidential hopeful.

Another benefit of an agreement plan is that it can work

to clarify shared values between our customers and us. Whole Foods' list of values has attracted millions to their stores and works as an agreement to source food in a way that is socially and environmentally responsible.

Unlike a process plan, an agreement plan often works in the background. Agreement plans do not have to be featured on the home page of your website (though they could be), but as customers get to know you, they'll sense a deeper level to your service and may realize why when they finally encounter your agreement plan.

The best way to arrive at an agreement plan is to list all the things your customer might be concerned about as it relates to your product or service and then counter that list with agreements that will alleviate those concerns.

If it's short enough (we're fans of brevity, obviously), you can feature your agreement plan on the wall of your business or even on your packaging or shopping bags.

WHAT'S THE PLAN CALLED?

Once you create your process or agreement plan (or both), consider giving each plan a title that will formalize the plan in the minds of your customers. For instance, your process plan might be called the "easy installation plan" or the "world's best night's sleep plan." Your agreement plan might be titled the "customer satisfaction agreement" or even "our quality guarantee." Titling your plan will frame it in the customer's mind and will increase the perceived seriousness of your offer and your commitment to customer satisfaction.

Now that you've given your customer a plan, they will be

much more likely to do business with you. You've lifted the fog, made the baby steps clear, and alleviated their concerns, and now they are ready to continue the journey.

Yet before many customers make a commitment, they will need one more thing from you. They will need you to call them to action. In other words, you're going to have to ask them for the money. Sadly, very few business leaders enjoy asking for the money, but that's because you're thinking of the transaction the wrong way. I'll teach you the right and wrong ways to call customers to action in the next chapter and, more importantly, I hope to transform you into somebody who boldly represents their brand with pride.

First, though, spend some time defining the plan or plans you want to implement to ease your customers' fears and guide them toward next steps.

CLARIFY YOUR MESSAGE SO CUSTOMERS LISTEN

- Go to StoryBrand.AI and either create a BrandScript or log in to your existing BrandScript.
- Either alone or with a team, brainstorm the simple steps a customer would need to take to do business with you (either a pre- or post-purchase process plan or a combination of both).
- What fears do your customers have related to your industry? What agreements could you make with your customers that would alleviate those fears?

- Do you share unique values with your customers? Can those values be spelled out in an agreement plan?
- Write the steps (and name) of your process plan on your StoryBrand BrandScript. If you're creating an agreement plan, simply use the notes section of your BrandScript to capture the agreement you'll be making with your customers.

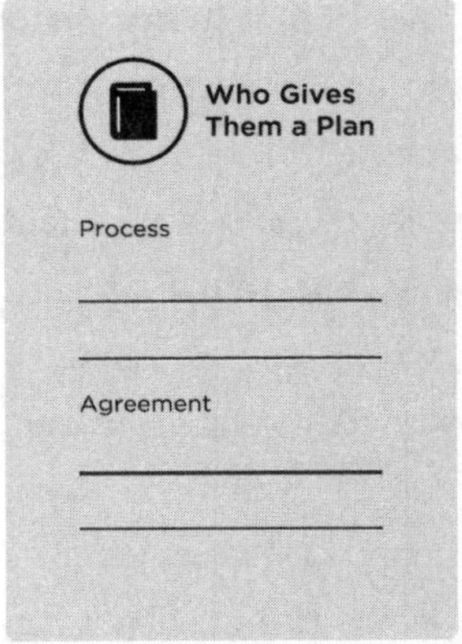

CHAPTER 8

AND CALLS THEM TO ACTION

StoryBrand Principle Five: Customers do not take action unless they are challenged to take action.

At this point in the story we are inviting our customer into, they are excited. We've defined a desire, identified their challenges, empathized with their frustrations, proved our competency, and given them a plan. But they still need us to do one more thing: they need us to call them to action.

ASK THEM TO PLACE AN ORDER

In stories, characters never take action on their own. They have to be challenged to take action. Tom Cruise's character would never have journeyed to pick up his brother in the movie *Rain Man* unless he'd received a call explaining his father had died.

Romeo wouldn't have climbed into the Capulet courtyard unless he'd fallen hopelessly in love with Juliet. Elle Woods wouldn't have applied to Harvard unless she'd been dumped by her boyfriend. Liam Neeson's character wouldn't have chased the bad guys to Europe unless his daughter had been kidnapped.

The reason characters have to be provoked into taking action is because everybody sitting in the dark theater knows human beings do not make major changes in their lives unless something challenges them to do so.

If I wrote a story about a guy who wanted to climb Everest and then one day looked at himself in the mirror and decided to do it, the audience would feel that something was wrong in the story itself. Making sudden decisions to change and then taking action on that decision is not how human beings operate. Bodies at rest tend to stay at rest, and so do customers. Heroes need to be challenged by outside forces.

Have you ever wondered why late-night infomercial hosts keep screaming, "Call now! Don't delay!" over and over as though they're trying to wake people up from a zombie trance? They do that because they're trying to wake people up from a zombie trance.

Your customers are bombarded with more than three thousand commercial messages per day, and unless we are bold in our calls to action, we will be ignored. If our calls to action are soft, they will not be noticed.

Do Not Put Customers in the Mind-Reading Business

A mentor once gave me terrific leadership advice that also applies to marketing and messaging: do not put people in the mind-reading business. He was emphasizing the need to communicate clearly. If you think people are able infer what you mean, you're mistaken. People who get what they want know how to ask in clear, simple language. And if you want customers to place an order, you, too, should ask using clear, simple language.

When it's time to ask for the order, we often use phrases like "If you're interested, let me know," but let's think about the passivity of that statement for a moment. Put yourself in the mind of the customer when they hear a statement like that. What ideas are they actually having to process subconsciously in response to that statement? *Am I interested? I'm not sure. How would I contact you? What happens if I'm not interested? Is there going to be weirdness between us if I decide not to buy? What if the product doesn't work for me? Why aren't you going to contact me? Why do I have to be the one who contacts you?* And the saddest thought that a customer could have is, *I'm ready to place an order now, but this guy wants me to contact him later. I hope I remember to do that.*

Next time you're closing a sale, try this statement instead: *If you're struggling with "X," which it sounds like you are, I think buying "Y" is the right decision. I can take your order now and you won't have to struggle with "X" anymore. Would you like to place an order right now?*

When I'm asked to speak to a group of sales professionals, I often ask the audience to pull out their laptops so we can write a sales email right there in the room. I ask them to hold up their hand if they have a client sitting on the fence, and of course every hand in the room goes up. I then walk them through a formula for a follow-up email using the SB7 framework, and we end with the call to action I just included for you above. Then, I tell the audience to hit "Send." Without exception, those emails have resulted in thousands and often millions in sales. In fact, the process works so well that my team and I guarantee that we will close more in sales during the training sessions themselves than we were paid to be there. We've never failed to deliver. In fact, the last time I guided a group of 250 account executives for a company called Calix, a growing broadband infrastructure and support provider for broadband services, through the process they closed more than 2.5 million in sales off the emails that went out during a single hour of the training. The CFO called my office a few days later to say he'd never seen anything like it in all his years in business. Why did that sales team close so many sales? Because the customers on the other end of those emails had experienced empathy and clarity about the problem they were facing and assurance that Calix's products would solve those problems. Those emails positioned the customer as the hero and the account executive as the guide, and they gave the client confidence that their story would end well. Plus, the calls to action were clear: Our product will solve your problem; would you like to place an order now?

The Power of the "Buy Now" Button

I have a friend who has bought and sold nearly one hundred companies. He knows a lot about scaling a business, and as he evaluates a company, he makes sure the people, products, and procedures are all healthy. But the key ingredient he looks for before he will buy a company is whether the sales process is correctly challenging their customers to place orders. Why? Because my friend knows the fastest way to grow a business is to make the calls to action clear and then repeat them over and over. He's made millions simply buying companies, creating stronger calls to action, and then selling those businesses after the revenue predictably increases.

One of the biggest hindrances to business success is wrongly assuming customers can read our minds. It's obvious to us that we want them to place an order (why else would we be talking to them about our products?), so we assume it's obvious to them too. It isn't.

Specifically, as it relates to marketing, there should be a "Buy Now" button in the top right corner of your website, and it shouldn't be cluttered with a bunch of other buttons. Your "Buy Now" button should be the obvious button to press, meaning it should be featured in a different font or a brighter color than the other buttons on the page. In short, your "Buy Now" or "Add to Cart" or "Schedule a Call" button should be the obvious button to press. The same call to action should be repeated above the fold and in the center of the header on your website, and then featured again and again as customers scroll down your page.

Companies that don't make their calls to action clear remind me of my dating days before I met my wife. Instead of clearly asking a girl out, I'd say something like, "If you ever want to get coffee, I'd be up for that. Do you like coffee?"

What in the world is a woman supposed to do with a question like that? That's just not how you make a baby.

As I got older I realized the power of clarity. In fact, the way my wife and I got together was probably the clearest I've communicated about anything. I'd known Betsy from a distance for a while, but when I finally got up the courage to ask her out, I discovered she had a boyfriend. Still, I'd been passive long enough. I'd been hoping she'd notice how much I liked her even as I doled out vague and passive hints. It was time for a strong call to action. The next time I saw her, I told her how I really felt and that I'd like to call her in thirty days to ask her out. I said she'd need to ditch the other guy to keep things from being awkward.

Amazingly, thirty days later, she was out of that relationship and we started dating. About a year later we got married. And now we have a baby. Turns out the StoryBrand framework is effective in a lot more than marketing, but I will save that for a later book.

The moral of the story is to make your call to action clear by asking customers a yes/no question. Statements like "If you're interested, let me know" do not prompt our customers to accept or reject our offer and instead send them off into a whirlwind of confusion. The chances of our customers going home, pouring a drink, and meditating on our vague offer are next to zero, so don't expect to close many sales if you're passive and confusing.

When I was a kid there was a guy on late-night television who used to saw mattresses in half with a chainsaw. He'd scream at the camera that he'd gone crazy and was slashing prices on all kinds of furniture. He was effective, but he also looked a little foolish. A lot of us are afraid to ask for the sale because we don't want to look like an infomercial pitch man, but very few people reading this book are ever going to come off as pushy. Of the thousands of clients we've worked with, we've yet to encounter anybody who oversells. Most people think they're overselling when, in truth, their calls to action fall softer than a whisper.

Do You Believe in Your Product?

When we try to sell passively, we communicate a lack of belief in our product. When we don't ask for the sale clearly, the customer senses weakness. When we are vague, our customers think we're asking them for charity rather than standing in the confidence that our product can change their lives. Customers aren't looking for brands that are filled with doubt and in need of affirmation; they're looking for brands that have solutions to their problems.

If we can change our customer's story for the better, why shouldn't we be bold about inviting them to do business with us? The guide in a movie must be direct about what they want the hero to do; otherwise, the guide comes off as weak and the audience experiences cognitive dissonance and loses interest.

Two Kinds of Calls to Action

At StoryBrand, we recommend two kinds of calls to action: *direct calls to action* and *transitional calls to action*. These calls to action work in two different phases of the guide/hero relationship.

Let's say we ask a customer to buy but they aren't ready. Who knows why, but they aren't ready. There's no reason to end the relationship just because they want more time. In fact, most customers, especially if the item is expensive or if the sales process is complicated, rightly need more time. If this is the case, we want to deepen the relationship so that whenever they are ready, they will remember us. The way I deepen that relationship is through transitional calls to action.

Direct calls to action include requests like "buy now," "schedule an appointment," or "call today." A direct call to action is something that leads to a sale or at least is the first step down a path that leads to a sale.

Transitional calls to action, however, do not require a

purchase but do require some sort of commitment that further builds toward a trusting relationship. Transitional calls to action can be used to "on-ramp" potential customers to an eventual purchase. Inviting people to watch a webinar or download a PDF are good examples of transitional calls to action.

To further the relational metaphor, a transitional call to action is like asking your customer, "Can I take you out on a date?" and a direct call to action is like popping the question, "Will you marry me?"

In our marketing collateral, we always want to have a direct call to action and a transitional call to action. A metaphorical conversation with our customers goes like this:

Us: Will you marry me?
Customer: No.
Us: Will you go out with me again?
Customer: Yes.
Us: Will you marry me now?
Customer: No.
Us: Will you go out with me again?
Customer: Sure, you're interesting and the information you provide is helpful. I will go out with you again.
Us: Will you marry me?
Customer: Okay, I'll marry you now.

As a brand, it's our job to pursue our customers. We want to get to know them and for them to get to know us, but we are the ones who need to take the initiative and keep the relationship alive and flourishing, even if they aren't ready to place an order.

THOSE WHO ASK AGAIN AND AGAIN SHALL FINALLY RECEIVE

Now that you've read this chapter, you will begin to notice how good brands build relationships, even using text on landing pages, lead generators, and emails. Years ago I was preparing a keynote presentation for a global shampoo brand and my graphic designer was too busy with other projects to help. Not wanting to wait, I decided to outsource the presentation to a design house. I went looking online for a shop that dealt specifically with presentations and found two local houses that could help.

The first website I visited was beautifully designed—including a looping video loaded beneath text that explained the design house's values and priorities. After about twenty seconds admiring the look of their site, though, I started searching for information about how to do business with them. I couldn't find anything. They featured samples of previous projects, a few testimonials, and a phone number I could call but no direct, clear call to action. So I decided to check out their competitor's site.

The other company's site wasn't nearly as beautiful, but it dared to be clear. "If you're worried about a presentation, we can help you hit a grand slam." The truth is I was worried about my presentation, and they spoke to my internal fear. They also painted a picture of a climactic scene: hitting a grand slam. Then they asked me out: They offered a PDF called "5 Things Great Presenters Get Right," and I was quite curious. I downloaded the PDF and read it in a few minutes. Their transitional call to action earned my trust and positioned them as the guide in my story. They had authority, it seemed, because in the lead generator they talked about all the other leaders they had helped. Then they sent me emails with helpful information about giving good keynotes. Each email would ask me to schedule a call, but for the first couple of weeks I ignored that request. After reading yet another helpful email, though, about two weeks out, I clicked on a link that took me back to their website. On their website, they had a clear and bright "Schedule a Call" button, and because they'd wined and dined me, I did. I scheduled a call. I never went back to the initial designer's website (which, remember, was much better looking) because, although they had an impressive-looking site, they'd failed to build a trusting relationship with me, and before long I was gladly writing a check for several thousand dollars to the company that had clearly built a relationship over time and then challenged me to take action.

Direct Calls to Action

It bears repeating: there should be one obvious button to press on your website, and that button should be the direct call to action. When I say, "one obvious button," I don't mean "only one button" but rather one that stands out.

Our customers should always know we want to marry them. Even if they're not ready, we should keep letting them know where we'd like the relationship to go. Customers don't buy when we are ready for them to buy; they buy only when two realities overlap: they realize they have a problem and they remember you have a solution. If they don't have a problem, they aren't going to place an order; if they do have a problem but forgot you have a solution, they will make a purchase from somebody else who had made the effort to ask them out, spend time with them, and build trust. You just never know when a customer is going to want to make a commitment, and when they do, you want to be on one knee, holding flowers, smiling for the picture.

Examples of direct calls to action are

- Order now
- Call today
- Schedule an appointment
- Register today
- Buy now

Direct calls to action can be included at the end of every email blast, on signage, in our radio ads, and even in our television commercials. Consider including direct calls to action in every team member's email signature and, if you really want to get the point across, on all your business cards. The idea is to make it very clear what we'd like customers to do: to make a purchase so we can help them solve their problem.

Transitional Calls to Action

Direct calls to action are simple and obvious (though ridiculously underused), but transitional calls to action can be equally as powerful to grow your business. In fact, StoryBrand grew into a multimillion-dollar company in only its second year based solely on the use of a transitional call to action. Recognizing that most of our clients were using the StoryBrand framework to fix their websites, we released a free PDF called "5 Things Your Website Should Include," and thousands of people downloaded it. At the back of the PDF we placed an ad for our StoryBrand Marketing Workshop. In the next twelve months, we doubled revenue on our workshops without spending a dollar on marketing.

A good transitional call to action can do three powerful things for your brand:

1. **Stake a claim to your territory.** If you want to be known as the leader in a certain territory, stake a claim to that territory before the competition beats you to it. Creating a PDF, a video series, or anything else that positions you as the expert is a great way to establish authority.
2. **Create reciprocity.** I've never worried about giving away too much free information. In fact, the more generous a brand is, the more reciprocity they create. All relationships are give-and-take, and the more you give to your customers, the more likely it is they will give something back in the future. Give freely.
3. **Position yourself as the guide.** When you help your customers solve a problem, even for free, you position yourself as the guide. The next time they encounter a problem in that area of their lives, they will look to you for help.

Transitional calls to action come in all shapes and sizes. Here are a few ideas to create transitional calls to action of your own:

- **Free information:** Create a white paper or free PDF educating customers about your field of expertise. This will position you as a guide in their story and create reciprocity. Educational videos, podcasts, webinars, and even live events are great transitional calls to action that on-ramp customers toward a purchase.
- **Testimonials:** Creating a video or PDF including testimonials from happy clients creates a vision of a climactic scene

in your customer's mind. When they see others experience a successful ending to their story, they will want that same ending for themselves.

- **Samples:** If you can give away free samples of your product, do it. Offering a customer the ability to test-drive a car, taste your seasoning, sample your music, or read a few pages of your book are great ways to introduce potential customers to your products.
- **Free trial:** Offering a limited-time free trial works as a risk-removal policy that also on-ramps your customers. Once they try your product, they may not be able to live without it.

Connecting the Dots

Earlier this year StoryBrand worked with a clinic that specialized in health screening, drug testing, treating minor sicknesses, and giving shots. The primary traffic the clinic received was through businesses who needed their employees to complete drug tests, which provided a steady stream of predictable revenue. Still, the clinic was stagnant in growth. Customers were coming in to get one product but weren't aware of anything else the clinic offered.

Upon visiting the clinic, one of our StoryBrand marketing coaches noticed they were missing a clear, direct, and transitional call to action.

Patients would come into the shop, sign and date an entry form, then sit in the lobby reading magazines or watching television while they waited for a nurse. As one of our StoryBrand certified coaches consulted with the clinic, she told the owner to remove the television and magazines. Instead, she encouraged them to create a transitional call to action called "The Healthy Body Checklist," allowing patients to self-assess their health. The checklist included questions like, "Do you feel tired at about two in the afternoon every day?" and "Are you satisfied with your current weight?" After patients finished their drug or blood tests, we suggested that nurses review the checklist with each patient and let them know about solutions that were also available at the clinic. The receptionist could then enter the customer's data into their email marketing system and, based on how a patient was tagged, an automated campaign would go into effect. If the customer seemed like they needed more vitamin B, they'd get a series of emails explaining the benefits of a monthly vitamin B shot, along with clear calls to action directing the patient to make another appointment. What happened? Sales, of course, increased. And why? Because the nurses provided a transitional call to action that identified the customer's problems and then the clinic built a trusting relationship with each new client via an automated email campaign.

Is there a transitional call to action you can create that will grow your business? Are your direct calls to action clear and repeated often? If not, your customers likely don't know what you want them to do. Remember, people are drawn to clarity and away from confusion. Having clear calls to action means customers aren't confused about the actions they need to take to do business with you, and having transitional calls to action increases the length and depth of the relationship you are building with customers.

WHAT ARE THE STAKES?

At this point in the optimizing of your messaging and marketing using the StoryBrand framework, customers are going to start placing orders. But let's not stop. How can we make the story we are inviting customers into so enticing that they can't wait to do business with us?

To do this, we must define the stakes. What's at stake in the customer's story if they do or do not choose to buy our product? If we've not defined the stakes, we've missed the opportunity to make the story interesting.

In the next two modules, I'll teach you how to increase a sense of intrigue and urgency with your brand by defining exactly what's at stake.

Before we move forward, though, continue clarifying your business by brainstorming potential calls to action you can include in your StoryBrand BrandScript.

CLARIFY YOUR MESSAGE SO YOUR CUSTOMERS LISTEN

- Go to StoryBrand.AI and either create a BrandScript or log in to your existing BrandScript.
- Decide what direct call to action you want to include in your marketing material.
- Brainstorm any transitional calls to action you can create that will stake a claim to your territory, create reciprocity

with your customers, further build a relationship, and position your brand as a guide.

- Fill out the "Call to Action" section of your StoryBrand BrandScript.
- *To learn more about our sales training, visit StoryBrandSalesTransformation.com*

And Calls Them to Action

Direct

Transitional

CHAPTER 9

THAT HELPS THEM AVOID FAILURE

StoryBrand Principle Six: Every human being is trying to avoid a tragic ending.

A story endears an audience based on its ability to gen-erate interest in a single question: Will the hero succeed or fail in accomplishing their objective? To encourage the audience to care about the hero and their objective, a good storyteller employs well-worn narrative tactics. For example, the first thing the storyteller must do is make the hero relatable and sympathetic: This is why so many stories begin by showing you how the hero became an orphan. Orphans are sympathetically endearing to every human being because orphans are almost always innocent creatures who are lost and in need of completion, which is a state humans find themselves in several times each week. All of us feel like orphans from time to time, even if we had terrifically attentive parents. To feel like an orphan, in the psychological sense, is to realize that your life is your own and in the end you're going to have to take responsibility for that life in your search for completion. In a meaningful narrative treatment, then, the completion the hero must find takes on a symbolic form of some sort, such as accomplishment (Daniel winning the karate tournament in *The Karate Kid*) or relational fulfillment (every romantic comedy you can think of) or a return to home (*Lord of the Rings* and all the *Benji* movies). In short, the storyteller's job is to make us care about the hero as long as it takes for the story to feel like a difficult and transformative journey. This is all fairly easy to accomplish by establishing an early hardship (a hero in a hole) and then stating a clear objective (the hero standing on the edge of the hole, reflecting back on how the journey changed them.) The hard job of the storyteller, though, is stretching it all out for ninety minutes or two hours or, in the case of a narrative series, several seasons on Netflix. So how do the storytellers elongate the plot so they can get a full-length feature out of the story idea? They interject conflict and then dangle high stakes.

In a previous chapter we talked about your customers' problems and how important it is to understand them and speak of them often. You will remember that the more you speak of your customers' problems, the more likely they are to buy your products. But speaking of your customers' problems will be twice as effective if you add one more element to your campaign—negative stakes.

In storytelling, narrative stakes are what's at play based on whether the hero accomplishes their objective. The higher a storyteller can raise the stakes, the more the audience leans in to find out what will happen.

Throughout a story, storytellers foreshadow a potential

successful ending and a potential tragic ending. The audience remains in suspense as long as the storyteller keeps the hero teetering on the precipice of success and failure. The key here is to use stakes in the story to shorten the audience's leash.

Need to raise the stakes in a romantic comedy? Have the young woman fall in love with the hero's brother, who, by the way, is a jerk and a bully and a con artist. Then, continue to show the bully brother reeling in the romantic interest through lies and deception, all the while making the audience cringe at how horribly this story might end. If the young woman marries the con artist brother, both her life and the life of the hero will be ruined. Of course, any time the storyteller needs to heighten a sense of urgency, they can simply pull on the "make the brother do something awful" lever and the audience will lean in even more.

Storytellers use stakes as plot devices all the time, and in our journey to clarify our brand's message, we can learn something from this proven tactic. The question we must then ask ourselves as we clarify our message is, What can be won or lost in our customers' lives if they do or do not purchase our products?

The only two motivated actions a hero can take in a story are to move away from something bad or move toward something good. Such is life. Our desire to avoid pain motivates us to seek a resolution to our problems.

If a storyteller doesn't clearly let an audience know what no-good, terrible, awful thing might befall their hero unless she overcomes her challenge, the story will have no stakes, and a story without stakes will lose favor with an audience—fast.

As a rule, each scene in a movie must provide a clear answer to the "stakes" question—that is, What's at stake in this scene for the hero? Every conversation, every chase scene, every sentimental and reflective montage should serve the movie in the same way: it must move the character either closer to or further from the tragic result that might befall them.

We kept turning the pages of Charlotte Brontë's *Jane Eyre* based on our suspicion that Edward Rochester was hiding something even darker than we first suspected.

We sat on the edge of our seats in the movie *Jaws* because we knew that more citizens of Amity Island might be killed by the shark if Chief Martin Brody didn't do something.

Imagine a story in which nothing bad could befall the hero. Imagine a love story in which everything went well for the couple straight through to the beautiful and tension-free wedding. Imagine an action movie in which the bomb the hero had to destroy was actually a dud and nobody was ever in actual danger. Would an audience care?

The lesson for those of us clarifying our brand message is this: brands that don't paint the stakes fail to answer the "so what" question every customer is secretly asking.

WHERE'S THE MAYHEM?

Allstate Insurance's long-running Mayhem campaign features dozens of commercials featuring actor Dean Winters humorously portraying various maladies such as raccoons in the attic or a raging fire started by a barbecue grill at a tailgating party. The idea is to humorously remind people why they need insurance. Mayhem, then, is always contrasted against the peaceful stability of life protected by Allstate, buttoned up with the reflective question, "Are you in good hands?"

In 2015, Allstate, along with the advertising agency Leo Burnett, took the campaign to a terrifically entertaining level. During the Sugar Bowl on New Year's Day, Allstate launched a campaign called Project Share Aware. The idea was to make people aware that sharing their whereabouts on social media might tip off criminals about when to burglarize their homes.

To announce the project, Allstate found a real couple and led them to believe they'd won a prize. They visited the couple in their home, secretly taking pictures of their household items. Later, they recreated their home on a soundstage, complete with duplicates of their belongings. The couple was then invited to attend the Sugar Bowl and given their own private box. During the game, Mayhem began auctioning off the couple's belongings on national television. People were directed to Mayhemsale.com for bargain-basement prices on everything from the couple's used car to an old tuba. As the couple watched their possessions being sold on the big screens at the game, hidden cameras caught their reactions and broadcast their actual panic on live television.

Of course, the couple's actual possessions were safe. Nevertheless, the campaign agitated a fear in many Americans. In fact, news outlets all over the country, including ABC News, *Wall Street Journal*, and the *New York Times*, covered the story. Suddenly, the threat of criminals walking into our homes as we announce our distant whereabouts on social media became a national fear.

The result of the campaign for Allstate? Mayhemsale.com received six to ten thousand hits per second immediately following each commercial. The site received more than eighteen million hits during the game. Also, #Mayhemsale trended in the top ten hashtags during the game, and immediately after the commercials aired, it surged to number one worldwide. Mayhem's X followers (then Twitter) increased by twenty-four thousand during the game, and the first commercial of the campaign resulted in more than twenty million impressions on Facebook and almost seventy thousand likes.[1] Allstate had, in the course of one football game, foreshadowed a potential failure (stakes) for their customers and sold an insurance product that would protect them, both opening a dark psychological story loop and offering a product to close it in a single campaign.

Of course, we don't all have access to the millions it takes to create a campaign like this, but the benefits of featuring the potential pitfalls of not doing business with us are much easier to include than we may think. Blog subjects, email content, and bullet points on our website can all include elements of potential failure to give our customers a sense of urgency when it comes to our products and services.

WHAT'S THERE TO LOSE?

As it relates to negative stakes in our marketing, the obvious question is, What will the customer lose if they don't buy our products?

Some of you just cringed. I understand. I used to cringe when I thought about "warning" my customers about imminent doom too. Why wouldn't I? The last thing I want to be is a fearmonger, because it's true that fearmongers can give customers the cringe. But fearmongering is not the problem 99.9 percent of business leaders struggle with. In our messaging, most of us actually generate the opposite dynamic in the minds of our customers because we don't define the negative stakes of the story we are inviting customers into, and this presents us as uninteresting. Remember, if there are no stakes in the story, there is no story.

In a good movie, you must be able to pause the screen and define what is at stake both in the overall story and in the specific scene itself. For instance, if we pause Jason Bourne midscene, we must be able to easily decipher that if he doesn't figure out who he is and who is out to get him, the mysterious bad guys will win and he will die, *and* if he doesn't get out of this house before the hit team shoots him, he will die here and now. In other words, there are stakes and then substakes at play from the first minute of the movie to the last.

The same must be true in your marketing and messaging. If I am perusing your landing page, I must know what the stakes are if I do or don't buy your product, and if you send me an email telling me about your product, there must be stakes in the email too. If you are giving me an elevator pitch, those stakes must be repeated. And by the way, if you are offering a lead-generating PDF, there must be stakes as to whether I download it; and if I do, there must be stakes as to whether I read it; and if I do read it, the stakes must be clear as to whether I buy your product and also whether I buy by midnight tonight. Too many stakes? Almost never. Can there be too many stakes in an action movie? And don't you want the story you are inviting customers into to be as engaging as an action movie?

Too many of our messaging campaigns play out with the slow-moving urgency of a French art film that has no commercial appeal save for the avant-garde, twenty-something wannabe-writer using the film to bolster their fragile artistic identity as a way to feel superior over others, despite the fact that it failed to attract the women they wanted and that the money they squandered producing it could have been better spent lining the tip jar of a good therapist. Speaking for a friend.

Human Beings Are Motivated by Loss Aversion

Emphasizing potential loss is more than just good storytelling; it's good behavioral economics. In 1979, Nobel Memorial Prize–winner Daniel Kahneman published a theory about why people make certain buying decisions. Prospect theory, as it is called, espoused that people are more likely to be dissatisfied with a loss than they are to be satisfied with a gain. In other words, people hate losing one hundred dollars more than they like winning one hundred dollars. The study proved that loss aversion is a greater motivator of buying decisions than potential gains. In fact, according to Kahneman, in certain situations, people are two to three times more motivated to make a change to avoid a loss than they are to achieve a gain.[2]

Loss aversion can be employed any time we need to convince people to make the right decision. When Lyndon Baines Johnson worked to pass the Civil Rights Act of 1964, he faced undying pressure from political leaders across the South. One of the principal leaders who refused to endorse the legislation was George Wallace, then governor of Alabama. Wallace had no vote on the bill, but his influence threatened its passage all the same. At a crucial moment in the negotiations, Johnson sat Wallace down and explained he'd better get on the right side of history. Johnson said that Wallace's legacy hung in the balance, that people would either build a statue in his honor or he'd be remembered for instigating hate. The choice was his. In other words, Johnson spelled out the narrative structure of his leadership effort and emphasized the stakes, including the potential of the governor's tarnished legacy. The civil rights bill, of course, was passed.

So how do we use messages from the failure category in our StoryBrand BrandScript? In Dominic Infante, Andrew Rancer, and Deanna Womack's book *Building Communication Theory*, they propose a four-step process called a "fear appeal."

First, we must make a reader (or listener) know they are vulnerable to a threat. I'll use a simple marketing narrative for a pest-control business as an example:

"Nearly 30 percent of all homes have evidence of termite infestation."

Second, we should let the reader know that since they're vulnerable, they should take action to reduce their vulnerability.

"Since termites will destroy your home, you should do something about it to protect your investment."

Third, we should let them know about a *specific* call to action that protects them from the risk.

"At ACME Pest Control, we offer a complete home treatment that will ensure your house is free of termites."

Fourth, we should challenge people to take this specific action.

"To enjoy a 10 percent discount, call us today and schedule your home treatment."[3]

Essentially, Infante, Rancer, and Womack present a soft way of agitating a fear and then highlight a path that would return readers or listeners to peace and stability, saving them from the negative stakes at play in the story.

The stakes in a story can be quite serious. If you are a doctor, stating the negative stakes clearly can save lives. Sure, you may disturb a patient or two as you explain that they need to change their diet or remember to take their medication, but isn't disrupting their comfort worth it if you are saving their lives?

Make no mistake, the words that describe negative stakes matter. If there is something serious at stake, state it clearly. Sometimes a warning may feel like bad news, but if that warning will prevent devastation, say it boldly.

Fear Is Salt in the Recipe

We do not need to use a great deal of fear in the story if we want to see results. Just a pinch of salt in the recipe will do. While we do need to communicate something from the failure category in order to complete our BrandScript, too many warnings about imminent doom will run the risk of turning customers off.

Infante, Rancer, and Womack explain why:

> When receivers of negative messaging are either *very* fearful or *very* unafraid, little attitude or behavior change results. High levels of fear are so strong that individuals block them out; low levels are too weak to produce the desired effect. Messages containing moderate amounts of fear-rousing content are most effective in producing attitudinal and/or behavior change.[4]

The lesson here is that we mustn't let a fear of negative messaging keep us from using it, because if we don't use negative messaging, our campaign will fail to stimulate action. That said, we can't overuse it either. In my view, though, almost nobody reading this book will overuse it. Instead, most of us will let our fear of negative messaging cause us to make the larger mistake, which is to use so little of it, or to keep the negative messaging so vague, that it fails to enhance our message and create urgency. For me, this is the general rule: when I am slightly uncomfortable with the negativity of my message, I add a little more and then stop. In my experience, my feeling that I'm being negative is shared only half by the person hearing the message.

Another truth to consider is that your negative message is mostly converted into a positive message if you're marrying those warnings with an offer of redemption. For instance, ask yourself if the following story is happy or sad:

> A man went into a bank with a gun and held ten people hostage, including a small child. The child cried as the man brandished the gun and yelled at the hostages to lay still. Police called in to the bank, but the robber would not answer the phone. It wasn't until the mother of the child began speaking to the robber, identifying with his frustrations about the unfairness of the economy and sympathizing with the robber's plight, that the robber let the hostages go and was later apprehended safely.

Do you read that as a sad story or a happy story? Most readers would say that the story is a feel-good story because it has a happy ending, yet the story is about a potentially violent criminal threatening the lives of the innocent, including a child. In fact, there are many more negative characteristics to the story than there are positive, yet the soft plot points of empathy and compassion and allowing the hostages to go free color the rest of the story. The principle is, the darker the story gets, the brighter the light is at the end of the tunnel.

As business leaders, it is important to understand that emphasizing the negative consequences in play only makes placing the order a more hopeful and happy conclusion. In other words, the bad makes the good even better.

WHAT ARE YOU HELPING YOUR CUSTOMER AVOID?

What negative consequences are you helping customers avoid? Could your customers lose money if they don't place an order? Are there health risks in play if your customers avoid your services? What about opportunity costs? Could they make or save more money with you than with a competitor? Could your customers' quality of life decline if they pass up your offer? What is the cost of not doing business with you?

If you're a financial adviser, for example, the list of what you're helping customers avoid might look like this:

- Confusion about how your money is being invested
- Not being ready for retirement
- A lack of transparency from your financial adviser
- A lack of one-on-one interaction with your adviser
- Hidden fees

In your marketing copy, you can even imagine a tragic scene that might befall your customers if they don't engage. In an email or on a landing page, a financial adviser might write something like this:

"Don't postpone your retirement. You've worked too hard for too long to not enjoy time with your grandchildren."

Here are a few examples of what StoryBrand clients are helping their customers avoid:

Perkins Motorplex (used cars)

- Getting ripped off by a used car salesman
- Being stuck with a lemon
- Feeling taken advantage of

Rely Technology (audio and video for the home)

- Living in a boring home
- Nobody will want to watch the game at your house
- You need a PhD to turn on your television

Aerospace Market Entry (manufacturer of aerospace equipment)

- Product failure, damaging your reputation
- Inefficient production
- Being passed by the competition

Win Shape Camps (summer camp for kids)

- A long, boring summer
- A bunch of restless kids in your house
- Regret about having wasted the summer

You can see how including these ideas in each client's marketing material gave the story they invited customers into a sense of intrigue and urgency.

In this module of your StoryBrand BrandScript, you're given only a few bullet points. You'll notice you're given a great deal more in the success module. This, of course, is on purpose. You'll need only a few terrible, dastardly, awful things to warn your customers about in order to create the necessary sense of urgency. Too much negativity and your customers will resist you, but if you use too little they won't know why your products even matter.

Once we've defined the negative stakes, your customers will be motivated to resist failure. In the next chapter, we'll dramatically increase their motivation by helping them imagine how great life could be once they buy your product or service. After your customers understand what you offer and how it can make their lives better, you'll have included stakes in the story you are inviting them into, and customer engagement will increase. First, though, let's warn customers about the consequences of not doing business with you.

CLARIFY YOUR MESSAGE SO CUSTOMERS LISTEN

- Go to StoryBrand.AI and either create a BrandScript or log in to your existing BrandScript.
- Brainstorm the negative consequences you are helping your customers avoid.
- Write down at least three of those consequences on your StoryBrand BrandScript.

CHAPTER 10

AND ENDS IN A SUCCESS

StoryBrand Principle Seven: Never assume people know how your brand can change their lives. Tell them.

Years ago, a friend gave me good leadership advice. He said, "Don, always remember, people want to be taken somewhere. Figure out where you want to take them and state it clearly, then repeat yourself over and over until you get them there."

I've found that advice applies to my family, my team, the books I write, and the speeches I give. And it certainly applies to my brand messaging.

Where is your brand taking people? Are you taking them to financial security? To the day when they'll move into their dream home? To a fun weekend with friends? Stories are about people who are going places, and, perhaps without knowing it, every potential customer we meet is asking us where our brand can take them.

Clarifying the message of your brand, at its core, is about leadership. The job of your brand is to guide the hero out of a hole and into a better life. And casting a vision might be the most important element in any leadership campaign. Ronald Reagan envisioned America as a shining city on a hill. Bill Clinton promised to build a bridge to the twenty-first century. Casting a clear, aspirational vision has always served a presidential candidate.

By foreshadowing a potential successful ending to a story, or, as Stew Friedman at the Wharton School puts it, defining a "compelling image of an achievable future,"[1] leaders captivate the imaginations of their audiences.

Successful brands, like successful leaders, make it clear what life will look like if somebody engages their products or services. Nike promised to bring inspiration and innovation to every athlete. Likewise, Starbucks offered to inspire and nurture their customers, one cup at a time. For years, Men's Wearhouse promised, "You're gonna like the way you look," and they even guaranteed it.

Without a vision, the people perish. And so do brands.

In the final and most important element of the StoryBrand framework, we're going to offer our customers what they want most: a happy ending to their story.

THE VISION SHOULD BE SPECIFIC AND CLEAR

One of the problems we run into with StoryBrand clients is the vision they paint for their customer's future is too fuzzy. Nobody gets excited about a muddled vision. Stories aren't vague, they're defined; they're about specific things happening to specific people. Otherwise they're not stories; they're just the telling of random events.

Harrison Ford had to defeat the terrorists in *Air Force One* to return to a peaceful White House. Erin Brockovich had to win the final verdict against Pacific Gas and Electric so the citizens of Hinkley, California, could be rightly compensated for their pain. In a good story, the resolution must be clearly defined so the audience knows exactly what to hope for.

Being specific matters. President Kennedy would have bored the world had he cast a vision for a "highly competitive and productive space program." Instead, he defined the ambition specifically and visually and as such inspired a nation: "We're going to put a man on the moon."

BEFORE AND AFTER

My friend Ryan Deiss at DigitalMarketer created a great tool to help us imagine the success our customers will experience if they use our products and services.

In a simple grid, Ryan allows us to see how our customers' lives will look after they engage us, how they will feel, what their average day will look like, and what kind of new status they will enjoy.

Filling out this grid for your brand will clarify the vision you have for your customers. Once you know how your customers' lives will change after they engage your brand, you will have plenty of effective copy to use in your marketing collateral.

	BEFORE YOUR BRAND	AFTER YOUR BRAND
What do they have?		
What are they feeling?		
What's an average day like?		
What is their status?		

The next step is to say it clearly. We must tell our customers what their lives will look like after they buy our products, or they will have no motivation to do so. We have to talk about the end vision we have for their lives in our keynotes, in our email blasts, on our websites, and everywhere else.

Images are also important when it comes to casting a vision for our customers. If you're selling kitchen flooring, your website might show a happy mom picking up her child from the beautiful and sparkling kitchen floor. If you're selling education, show us students in the classroom having a great time learning in the environment you provide. Regardless of what you sell, if possible, show us people happily engaging with your product.

HOW THE STORY ENDS MATTERS

Ultimately, the success module of your StoryBrand BrandScript should solve all three levels of your customers' problems: external, internal, and philosophical. As you contemplate the vision you will cast for the story you're inviting customers into, consider what their life will look like when they solve the physical problem, then think about how that resolution will make them feel, then consider why the resolution to their problem has made the world a more just place for them. When we resolve our customers' external, internal, and philosophical problems, we've truly envisioned an appealing resolution to their story and have increased the chances they will step into that story.

To make a story satisfying to an audience, storytellers often work hard to resolve all three levels of the hero's conflict in what's called an obligatory (or climactic) scene. If written well, the scene happens just before the end of the movie, usually about nine minutes before the credit rolls. It's referred to as the obligatory scene because the storyteller is "obligated" to make it happen. If, for instance, a man meets a woman and falls in love in act 1, the storyteller is obligated to bring them together at the end (that is, if the storyteller is trying to make us feel good). The key to a stellar ending, though, is to successfully open the external, internal, and philosophical story loops early in the story and then close them all through a single event at the end.

Here's an example: At the end of George Lucas's film *Star Wars: A New Hope*, Luke Skywalker resolves the external conflict (he must destroy the Death Star by shooting a proton torpedo through the exhaust valve of the Death Star), his internal conflict (the persistent doubt that he has what it takes to be a Jedi), and the philosophical conflict (good versus evil as depicted by himself being pursued by the violent Darth Vader) in a single shot. When Luke lands the shot (spoiler alert), all three levels of conflict are resolved at once, giving the audience three levels of satisfaction and causing me, at the age of nine, to stand on my seat and throw popcorn into the air, much to my mother and sister's embarrassment.

Consider the end of David Seidler and Tom Hooper's Oscar-winning movie *The King's Speech*. The end of that movie utilizes the same narrative device as Lucas's *Star Wars*, and to the same stellar result. If King George VI is going to inspire the British people to stay in the fight and win the war against Hitler, the king must deliver a speech without a stutter (external problem), a task that has forced him to face his own struggling self-confidence (internal conflict). The stakes are high. Should he fail, Hitler's Nazis will conquer all of Europe on their way to world domination (good versus evil). Much to the audience's pleasure, of course, he delivers the speech perfectly and thus resolves all three levels of conflict in a single event of narrative harmony. Cue the Oscar music.

The strategy for your brand, then, is to spend your marketing copy opening external, internal, and philosophical story loops and then offer to resolve them through the use of your product. For example, here's a bit of sample copy for a fictional toothpaste company:

> You want a bright smile but are concerned about the harmful effects of fluoride in most toothpastes. You know you shouldn't have to compromise your health just to brush your teeth, so you've been looking for a better alternative. When you brush your teeth with Gel Fresh, though, you get clean teeth without the harmful effects and will feel better about how you're taking care of your teeth and yourself. You shouldn't

have to compromise your health just to have a great smile.

Let's break down this climactic scene as it relates to brand messaging:

External: I need to clean my teeth.
Internal: I feel bad about what fluoride might be doing to my health.
Philosophical: I shouldn't have to use a toothpaste that is bad for my body.

If we have successfully opened up the three levels of story loops in our messaging, then writing an ending to our customers' story is simple: when you brush your teeth with Gel Fresh, you get clean teeth without the harmful effects (external) and will feel better about how you're taking care of your teeth (internal) because you shouldn't have to compromise your overall health just to have a great smile (philosophical).

HERE ARE MORE WAYS TO STICK THE LANDING

If you want to take the idea of sticking the landing a little further, it's worth exploring how stories are resolved by narrative experts. After a good storyteller closes the three open story loops in a single scene, the hero steps into a new reality framed by an external or internal resolution (or both) that represents a new world.

The three dominant ways storytellers paint this new world are by providing the hero with

1. greater power or position,
2. unity with somebody or something that represents their wholeness, and
3. an experience of self-realization that also makes them whole.

What's important for us as we clarify our brand message is this: the fact that these are the three most-employed resolutions in popular stories implies these are three dominant psychological desires shared by most human beings.

If our brand can promise a resolution that associates with one of these driving desires, our BrandScript will be even more enticing.

This is important, so let's explore these three primal desires more closely:

1. Winning Power and Position (The Need for Status)

When I was in high school, a film came out called *Can't Buy Me Love* in which a likable loser named Ronald Miller falls in love with a popular cheerleader named Cindy Mancini. Unfortunately for me, in the script, Ronald's character was so overlooked in his school that most of the other characters in the movie accidentally called him Donald. You can imagine the teasing I received.

But we loved the movie all the same. Why? Because in the end, of course, Ronald gets the girl. But he gets more than the girl. He gains status. After winning Cindy's heart, he becomes one of the popular kids, or, more accurately, he realizes trying to be somebody else is a waste of time, which, of course, makes him more popular.

Regardless, it's a universal human desire to want status, which is evidenced by the number of "coming of age" stories in which a character realizes they've got what it takes to run with the big dogs. Even those who convince themselves they do not want status often want the status that comes with not wanting status.

As I mentioned earlier in the book, the primary function of our brain is to help us survive and thrive, and status, by some, can be perceived as gaining more security in a tribe or society. If our brand, then, can help our customers become more esteemed, respected, and appealing in a social context, we are likely offering something they want.

So how can our brand offer status? Here are four ideas:

Offer access: My wife loves using her Starbucks membership card because it gains her points, which gains her status and the occasional free latte. We've had many conversations about the intangibility of said status, but I've learned not to argue. She's excited to be on her way to some kind of double-pump jazzy diamond level, which I'm pretty sure means she can cut in front of people at the drive-through.

Create scarcity: Offering a limited number of a specific item creates scarcity, and owning something that is scarce is often seen as a status symbol. When Jeep puts a badge that reads "limited" on the back of their Grand

Cherokee, they're promoting the scarcity of that particular packaging of the luxury SUV, thus making it more desirable.

Offer a premium: Most companies earn 70 percent or more of their revenue from a small percentage of their clients. Few, though, identify those clients and offer them a title such as "Preferred" or "Diamond Member." I love being an "Emerald Club" member with National Car Rental because it means I get to bypass the counter, jump in a car, and drive off. We even recommend a status-associated title for the nonprofit brands we work with. People will be much more likely to donate if they know they are an "Anchor Donor" and even more likely if they get special privileges like updates from the founder or access to other donors at special, elite-level fundraisers.

Offer identity association: Premium brands like Mercedes and Rolex sell status as much as they do luxury. Is it worth it? Depends on who you ask. Status really does open doors, and by associating their brand (and thus their customers) with success and refinement, they offer the sort of status that may make others esteem or even envy them.

2. Union That Makes the Hero Whole (The Need for Something External to Create Completeness)

Another way to offer a satisfying resolution is for your brand to offer some kind of perceived completeness. The reason stories often end with the union of lovers has little to do with the desire for love or sex. Rather, union between male and female characteristics in a story symbolizes the achievement of completeness.

When the prince rescues the princess and the two characters unite at the end of the story, the audience witnesses what they subconsciously consider the joining of two halves. The subconscious idea is that the man needs to be tamed and the woman needs provision and protection in order for the two to become "whole," and in this context, "whole" really means safe and/or useful in the context of a family-building unit, which is tied to survival in the sense that it's the safest way to contribute to the continuation of our species. Traditional though it may seem, the formula works for most moviegoing audiences. This same popular formula is used in a million or more love songs and, in its opposite form, the million or more empathetic rants belted out by those who aren't getting any.

This need to be completed by an external source doesn't have to include a wedding or even a male or female character, however. Many buddy comedies use the same formula. Arnold Schwarzenegger comically portrays a more feminine, refined personality compared to his rough-and-tumble brother played by Danny DeVito in the hit comedy *Twins*. The principle, however, is the same: two likable but different characters come together to form a complete unit in order to accomplish a specific survival objective.

The controlling idea of this kind of ending is that the character is made complete (or equipped to defeat a foe) by somebody or something outside themselves. In love stories, of course, it's all about the union of male and female characteristics, but the emotional need this kind of story delivers is much greater. These stories are about being made whole by external provision.

So what are some of the ways we can offer external help for customers looking to become complete? Here are a few examples:

Reduced anxiety: For years, brands that sell basic items like dish detergent and glass cleaner have almost comically positioned their products as anti-anxiety medication. The hero in the commercial starts out in anxiety, raising their hands to the heavens, questioning God about the meaning of life because the grease won't come off their casserole dish. As the hero in the commercial uses the new dish detergent, his or her sense of frustration subsides until, at last, they're able to see their bright, shining face glowing back at them in the polished platter, and then off they go into the sunset. What is the brand really offering? Satisfaction for a job well done? A feeling of closure about a clean dish? A better, more peaceful life? All of the above. Will the use of your product lead to the relief of stress and a feeling of completeness? If so, talk about it and show it in your marketing material.

Reduced workload: Customers who don't have the right tools must work harder because they are, well, incomplete. But what if a tool you offer could give the customer what they're missing? Whether they're selling wheelbarrows, software, jackhammers, or a fishing apparatus, manufacturers have been positioning tools as "the thing that will make you superhuman" for decades. In this instance, consider your brand not unlike the character Q in the James Bond films. Your customer comes into your secret cave and explains their objective, and you reveal all the tools you offer.

More time: For many customers, time is scarce, and if our product can expand time, we're offering to solve an external problem that is causing an internal frustration.

> Not being able to "fit it all in" is often perceived by our customers as a personal deficiency. Any tool, system, philosophy, or even person who can expand time may offer a sense of completeness.

The list, of course, could go on for pages. The only question you need to ask if you're wanting to offer a satisfactory resolution to your customer's story is, How does my customer feel incomplete and how can my product be positioned to offer that completion? If you ask and answer this question in a short, simple way, you're looking at a terrific messaging sound bite.

3. Ultimate Self-Realization or Acceptance (The Need to Reach Our Potential)

Movies like *Rudy*, *Hoosiers*, and *Chariots of Fire* all tap into the human desire to reach the utmost of our human potential. And it's not just sports movies. *Legally Blonde*, *The Theory of Everything*, and *Whiplash* are all about heroes who face significant challenges in their journey to prove themselves. The desire to be more fuels the plot. Once proven, the heroes realize an inner peace and can finally accept themselves, not only because they've reached their potential but because they've learned to respect themselves along the way.

An outward demonstration of worth isn't always necessary to create this kind of resolution. Heroes can also take an internal journey to arrive at the same conclusion. When Bridget Jones realizes she is too good for the boss with whom she desired a relationship, she came to an ultimate self-realization that she is "worthy" and thus arrived at a state of stability. And while it's true she didn't close the story loop of uniting with the man she wanted, resolution is brought about as she abandons that goal in exchange for the greater fulfillment of self-acceptance and contentment.

In 2013, the soap company Dove released a series of short films featuring women who sat to be sketched by an FBI-trained forensic artist. Without actually seeing the women, the artist would draw each woman based on how she described herself. Later, the artist would draw the same woman based on how a stranger described her. The reveal was shocking. The sketches drawn from the stranger's description were always more beautiful than the ones in which the women described themselves. The point: many women don't realize how beautiful they are. The ad was an attempt to help women accept themselves and find greater contentment in their intrinsic beauty. Dove acted as the guide helping the hero transform.

Whether it's by fulfilling some purpose or accepting themselves as they are, this offer to return our hero to contentment fulfills a universal human desire: self-acceptance.

How can a brand offer self-acceptance? Here are a few ideas:

Inspiration: If an aspect of your brand can offer or be associated with an inspirational feat, open the floodgates. Brands like Red Bull, *Harvard Business Review*, Under Armour, The Ken Blanchard Company, Michelob Ultra, and even GMC have associated themselves with athletic and intellectual accomplishment and thus a sense of self-actualization.

Acceptance: Helping people accept themselves as they are isn't just a thoughtful thing to do; it's good marketing. Not unlike the Dove campaign, American Eagle turned heads when they launched their Aerie campaign. In the campaign, American Eagle used real people as models and refused to retouch the images. Tackling body-image issues, American Eagle went beyond basic product promotion and contributed to universal self-acceptance among their clientele.

Transcendence: Brands that invite customers to participate in a larger movement offer a greater, more impactful life. TOMS Shoes built a name for themselves by selling stylish shoes while simultaneously giving a pair to somebody in need in what they called a "one for one" model. Those who wore the shoes claimed a major factor in deciding to make the purchase was a sense of involvement with a larger movement. At less than ten years old, the for-profit brand sold for more than $700 million. Another example of a brand that helps customers achieve a level of transcendence is Daymond John's clothing brand FUBU, an acronym for "For Us By Us," in reference to the African American community being represented in the marketplace. The brand offered more than fashion; it offered a sense of unity, transcendence, and entrepreneurialism for the African American community. FUBU has earned more than $6 billion to date.

CLOSING THE STORY LOOPS

The idea behind the success module in the SB7 framework is that our sound bite, in this category, offers to close a story loop. Human beings are looking for resolutions to their external, internal, and philosophical problems, and they can achieve this through, among other things, status, self-realization, self-acceptance, and transcendence. If our products can help people achieve any or all of these things, we should make this clear in our StoryBrand BrandScript.

KEEP IT SIMPLE

Offering to close a story loop is much simpler than you think. Even the inclusion of smiley, happy people on your website is a strong way to depict the potential closing of a story loop. People want to be happy, and images of happy people hint that your product will deliver.

If you sell rugs, a successful resolution might look like a beautiful room or be captured in the sound bite "a room that finally feels finished." If you sell ice cream, a successful resolution might be "a rich, creamy taste of heaven." Do you sell camping gear? Here's a sound bite for your product tags: "always prepared for adventure."

While I've been slightly philosophical in this chapter, try not to overthink it. What problem are you resolving in your customer's life, and what does that resolution look like after they buy your product? Stick to basic answers because they really do work. Then, when you get good, strong sound bites, start diving deeper into the levels of problems your brand resolves. You don't need to think about external, internal, and philosophical sound bites at first. Just give me a sound bite that screams resolution, then sharpen the language as you refine your marketing message.

The important idea in this section is that we need to

repeatedly show how our product or service can make somebody's life better. If we don't tell people where we're taking them, they won't follow. A story has to go somewhere.

Have you told your customers what sort of life you want to guide them into?

Next, let's take a look at the biggest motivator your customer has for making a purchase: the desire to become somebody different. Before that, though, brainstorm your sound bites for the success element of your StoryBrand BrandScript.

CLARIFY YOUR MESSAGE SO CUSTOMERS LISTEN

- Go to StoryBrand.AI and either create a BrandScript or log in to your existing BrandScript.
- Brainstorm the successful resolution you're helping your customers achieve. What will their lives look like if they use your products and services?
- Use the bullet points in the success module of your BrandScript to capture your best answers.

CHAPTER 11

PEOPLE WANT YOUR BRAND TO PARTICIPATE IN THEIR TRANSFORMATION

Even though you've filled out the principal elements of your StoryBrand BrandScript, you've likely noticed there's one element left. This final element will serve as an overall character arc for your customer's journey. In fact, as we've discussed what your hero wants, what their challenges are, and what positive resolution your brand can provide, we've only danced around the greatest motivation your customer has to place an order. This single motivating factor is the secret driving force behind nearly every decision we make as human beings. Whether we're buying lawn furniture or choosing a mate, we can't escape a certain deep desire.

I'm talking about the human desire to *transform*.

Everybody wants to change. Everybody wants to be somebody

different, somebody better, or, perhaps, somebody who simply becomes more self-accepting. This desire for transformation is by design. Humans start as tiny babies, learning color and smell and sound and attachment. As we grow, we begin playing games in which we are animals or warriors or princesses or wizards. From the beginning, we long to grow and change and adapt and develop. This desire, by the way, never stops, all the way to our final days. And while we can't become wizards, we do want to become better and better versions of ourselves. Brands who offer to participate in this universal and deep-rooted desire and who are successful in delivering an aspirational identity often create brand evangelists.

Ever wonder how Taylor Swift created such raving fans? Her music is only part of the story. Mostly, young women identified with her strength, her ease, her willingness to share, her generosity, and, well, her identity. In short, she stands as a person many young women would like to become, and that isn't a bad thing. The same could be said for many of our sports heroes, our favorite actors and comics, and even many world leaders. Our subconscious minds are always looking for examples of who we want to be, and when we find one of those examples, our primitive brains, in small ways, have trouble differentiating themselves from ourselves. Why else do people get so defensive when you diminish their heroes? In their minds, you aren't just diminishing a public figure; you're diminishing the part of them that has attached their identity to that public figure. You're not just insulting Taylor Swift; you're insulting millions of people who want to be (and perhaps are) like Taylor Swift. If you don't believe me, just open your favorite social media app and comment about how you aren't sure Taylor made the right choice in shoes today. You will quickly be hung in the town square and your body will be dragged through the streets by teens leading teams of rhinestone-clad show horses.

Changing the subject in the name of personal safety, when you look closely at your StoryBrand BrandScript, you'll see the character arc already taking shape. Your brand really is helping people become better versions of themselves, which is a beautiful thing. You are helping your customers become wiser, more equipped, more physically fit, more accepted, and more at peace. Like it or not (and we hope you like it), we are all participating in our customers' transformation, which is exactly what they want us to do.

Again, brands that participate in the transformation of their customers' identity create passionate brand evangelists. Want critics to be hung in the town square and dragged through the street by teams of My Little Ponies when people disparage your brand? Keep reading.

THE DESIRE TO TRANSFORM RUNS DEEP

At the beginning of a story, the hero is usually flawed, filled with self-doubt, and ill-equipped for the task set before them. Faced with unbounded conflict, they meet a mysterious but competent guide who aids them on their journey. The conflict then begins to strengthen the character. Forced into action, the hero develops skills and accrues the experience needed to defeat their foe. Though the hero is still filled with doubt, they summon the courage to engage the fight and, in the climactic scene, defeat the villain, proving once and for all that they have changed and that they are now competent to face challenges as better versions of themselves, revealing that all along the story was about character transformation.

This same character arc, by the way, appears in *The Old Man and the Sea*, *Pride and Prejudice*, *Pinocchio*, *Hamlet*, *Sleeping Beauty*, *Swan Lake*, *Tommy Boy*, and thousands of other popular stories. Why? Because it's our story. Feelings of self-doubt are universal, as is the desire to become somebody competent and courageous. And all of this matters when it comes to the messages we create to brand our products and services.

As it relates to creating identify-transformation sound bites, a few important questions can prompt effective answers: Who does our customer want to become? What kind of person do they need to be to resolve their conflict? What characteristics would effectively describe our customer's aspirational identity?

SMART BRANDS DEFINE AN ASPIRATIONAL IDENTITY

Recently I ran down to Home Depot to get a stud finder so I could install shelving in the garage. Next to the stud finders in the tool section was a selection of Gerber knives. Gerber is a knife company out of Portland, Oregon, that makes a range of multipurpose pocketknives. Their commercial campaign, however, offers the buyer a lot more than a knife. They sell something intangible. They sell an identity, and by that I mean they sell an association with a kind of person you and I can become. I'd been noticing Gerber commercials for a long time, and even though I knew exactly what they were doing to my subconscious,

I wanted one anyway. *But why?* I thought to myself as I stood there staring at the knives. *I'm a writer. The only thing I need a knife for is to make a peanut butter and jelly sandwich.*

Still, the pull was palpable. What if I had to swim under a boat to cut away a tangled rope from the propeller? Or slice a pant leg off my bloody jeans to make a tourniquet for my injured arm? What if Taylor Swift fans stuffed me into a burlap sack and threw me off a pier? Couldn't I use the knife to cut my way out?

Thankfully, my executive brain overpowered my primitive brain, and I walked away with just the stud finder. But why was it so hard? Why did I want the knife so badly? And why did I change my mind and go back to buy the knife anyway? Certainly they make great knives, but there are many other companies making great knives and I'd never really cared or noticed.

The reason I wanted the knife is simple. Gerber defined an aspirational identity for their customers and then associated their product with that identity. The aspirational identity of a Gerber knife customer is tough, adventurous, fearless, action-oriented, and competent to do a hard job. Epitomized in their advertising campaign Hello Trouble, a Gerber customer is positioned as the kind of person who sails boats into storms, rides bulls, rescues people from floods, and yes, cuts tangled ropes from boat propellers. In their television commercials they present images of these aspirational, heroic figures cast over anthemic music and a narrator reciting the lines:

> Hello, Trouble.
> It's been a while since we last met.
> But I know you're still out there.

And I have a feeling you're looking for me.
You wish I'd forget you, don't you, Trouble?
Perhaps it's you that has forgotten me.
Perhaps I need to come find you,
  remind you who I am.[1]

The commercial is terrific. One day, to my surprise, a StoryBrand alumnus, who happens to be one of the Army Rangers about whom the movie *Black Hawk Down* was made, stopped by the house. We caught up for a moment, and then he gave me a little thank-you present, a Gerber knife. He even had my name engraved on the blade. He knew I liked the commercial and so offered it as a gift. To this day I keep that knife clipped to the dashboard of my 1978 FJ40 Land Cruiser. Occasionally I'll take the knife into the house, stare at a jar of peanut butter, and say, "Hello, Trouble."

I may be just a writer, but I love that knife.

But let me ask you a question. Was the knife I bought a waste of money? I mean, let's say I did pay forty dollars for the knife and never used it. Did I get ripped off?

I've asked that question to hundreds of people who are familiar with the StoryBrand messaging framework, and the answer has always come back the same: no. It was not a waste of money. It was well worth the forty dollars. I can't help but agree. The truth is when I buy a Gerber knife I get something more than a knife. In a way, Gerber helped me become a better person. They defined an aspirational identity and invited me to step into that identity. The knife made me feel more tough and adventurous, and they even created a moment between two friends. And that's worth a great deal more than forty dollars.

HOW DOES YOUR CUSTOMER WANT TO BE DESCRIBED BY OTHERS?

The best way to define an aspirational identity that our customers may be attracted to is to consider how they want their friends to talk about them. Think about it. When others talk about you, what do you want them to say? How we answer that question reveals who it is we'd like to be.

It's the same for our customers. As it relates to your brand, how does your customer want to be perceived by their friends and family? And can you help them become that kind of person? Can some aspect of your product participate in your customer's identity transformation? If you offer executive coaching, your clients may want to be seen as competent, generous, and disciplined. If you sell sports equipment, your customers likely want to be perceived as active, fit, and successful in their athletic pursuits.

Once we know who our customers want to be, we will have language to use in emails, blog posts, and all manner of messaging collateral.

A GUIDE OFFERS MORE THAN A PRODUCT AND A PLAN

Playing the guide is more than a marketing strategy; it's a position of the heart. When a brand commits itself to helping customers define their heroic ambition; resolve their external, internal, and philosophical problems; and inspire them with an aspirational identity, they do more than sell products—they change lives. And leaders who care more about changing lives than they do about selling products tend to do a good bit of both.

Last year StoryBrand consulted with Dave Ramsey and his team. Ramsey Solutions may be the best example of a narrative-based company I know, and Dave himself is a terrific example of a guide. Over a series of workshops, dinners, and speeches, we introduced the Ramsey team to the SB7 framework, less as a way of educating them than as a way of giving vocabulary to what they were already doing.

Dave Ramsey hosts one of the largest radio shows in America with more than eight million daily listeners. On the show he offers financial advice and strategies that revolve around tackling and conquering personal debt. Unlike many advisers, though, Ramsey offers more than wisdom; he offers a narrative map his customers can enter into. He comes back from every break on his radio show with the same line: "Welcome back to *The Dave Ramsey Show*, where debt is dumb, cash is king, and the paid-off home mortgage has taken the place of the BMW as the status symbol of choice." There they are, the elements of story, complete with an identity to step into and a new status symbol to go along with that new identity.

Though Dave's face is prominent on book covers and billboards promoting his show, he never positions himself as the hero. Instead, Ramsey has a near obsession with his listeners' stories. Dave's understanding of his listeners' external problems (consumer debt and financial illiteracy), internal problems (confusion and a feeling of hopelessness), and their philosophical problem (credit card companies don't care about your financial well-being and will gladly sell you debt you can't afford) engages listeners in a living story. Always entertaining, Dave never misses an opportunity to embolden his listeners with an aspirational identity, encourage their progress, and remind them that tackling their financial challenges offers them a leap toward personal transformation.

To cap it off, Dave offers a brilliantly placed climactic scene in his customers' story. After listeners execute a plan he offers through his Financial Peace University, they are invited on his show to perform a "Debt-Free Scream." People travel from thousands of miles away to be featured on the show, and when they arrive, dozens of the Ramsey team surround the accomplished heroes with applause as the heroes shout, "We're debt-free!"

Once a listener has completed the journey, Dave lets them know they've changed, that they are different now, and that there is nothing they can't accomplish if they apply themselves.

GREAT BRANDS OBSESS ABOUT THE TRANSFORMATION OF THEIR CUSTOMERS

When we first met with Dave, I was surprised to learn he didn't know that affirming the hero's transformation was an oft-included scene at the end of many stories. I mean, he knew it intuitively but had never noticed it as a plot point in hundreds of stories. After the climactic scene (the debt-free scream), the guide often comes back to affirm the transformation of the hero, telling them that they are now a different and better person.

At the end of *Star Wars: A New Hope*, the ghost of Obi-Wan stands next to Luke Skywalker as he's rewarded for bravery. In *The King's Speech*, Lionel tells King George he will be a great king. Peter Brand sits Billy Beane down in the movie *Moneyball* and lets him know he's hit the equivalent of a home run as the manager of the A's.

The main purpose these scenes serve is to mark the transformation the hero has experienced so the audience has a point of reference that contrasts the hero's character from the story's beginning. The audience needs to be told very clearly how far the hero has come, especially since the hero usually struggles with crippling doubt right up until the end and they don't even realize how much they have changed.

The principle here is this: A hero needs somebody else to step into the story to tell them they've transformed. Heroes do not realize their transformation intuitively. They must be told by somebody else, and that somebody is the guide. That somebody is you.

There are hundreds of thousands of financial advisers, and thousands of them have written books. Hundreds of those who've written books have podcasts or radio shows, and yet Dave Ramsey enjoys a wider popularity. Why? Well, certainly his advice is good. Nobody is attracted to incompetence. But I'm convinced it is the way he frames the customer's journey as a narrative and participates in and then affirms their transformation that sets him apart. Also, his messaging is clear: short, simple sound bites. And he has been repeating those sound bites for years.

IDENTITY TRANSFORMATION

In the final module of your StoryBrand BrandScript, we've included a section that will allow you to define an identity transformation your customer may experience as they relate to your brand.

Who does your customer want to become as they engage your products and services?

At StoryBrand, we want our customers to become clear and precise communicators. When customers finish this book or conclude their time with one of our StoryBrand certified coaches, we want them to return to the office and have people wondering what happened to them. How did they become so messaging savvy? How did they become so clear in their thinking? Why are their messaging ideas so good? Did they suddenly get a PhD in persuasion?

Similar to the success module of your StoryBrand BrandScript, the aspirational identity section answers a question about how the story ends, except instead of telling us where the story is going, it tells us who the hero has become.

Brands that realize their customers are human, filled with emotion, driven to transform, and in need of help truly do more than sell products; they change people. Dave Ramsey changes people. Apple changes people. TOMS Shoes changes people. Gerber knives changes people. It's no wonder brands like these have such passionate fans and do so well in the marketplace.

The statement you want to finish in order to define an identity transformation for your customer is this: We help our customers go from "X" to "Y." Let me explain.

EXAMPLES OF IDENTITY TRANSFORMATION

Thousands of StoryBrand clients have defined an aspirational identity for their customers and begun to participate in their transformation. Because of this, more and more companies are not just improving the world through their products and services; they're actually improving the way their customers see themselves. Offering an aspirational identity adds enormous value to everything else that we offer.

Here are some examples of aspirational identities from StoryBrand clients like you:

PET FOOD BRAND
From: Passive dog owner
To: Every dog's hero

FINANCIAL ADVISER
From: Confused and ill-equipped
To: Competent and smart

SHAMPOO BRAND
From: Anxious and glum
To: Carefree and radiant

Have you thought about who you want your customer to become? Participating in your customer's transformation can give new life and meaning to your business. When you identify an aspirational identity for your customers, your brand will not only transform customers but will begin to inspire and unite your own team. When your team realizes they sell more than products, that they guide people toward a stronger belief in themselves, their work will have greater meaning.

Spend some time thinking about who you want your customers to become. How can you improve the way they perceive themselves?

How can your brand participate in your customer's identity transformation?

CLARIFY YOUR MESSAGE SO CUSTOMERS LISTEN

- Go to StoryBrand.AI and either create a BrandScript or log in to your existing BrandScript.
- Brainstorm the aspirational identity of your customer. Who do they want to become? How do they want to be perceived by others?
- Use the "to" lines of your BrandScript to define an aspirational identity. Filling out the "from" line is then simple. It's simply the opposite of whatever you define as their aspirational identity captured in the "to" line.

CHAPTER 12

DEFINE YOUR CONTROLLING IDEA

Congratulations, you now have a StoryBrand BrandScript, which means you have seven categories of sound bites you can repeat over and over to grow your business. Trust me, you will be pleased at how quickly and how much these sound bites cause customers to pay attention to your brand. Orders will go up.

After taking tens of thousands of businesses through the StoryBrand framework, though, I realized there was one element missing from the old BrandScript. I've added this element into the new BrandScript because I think it's that important. In fact, this specific sound bite is so important that if you create only this one bit of copy I believe it will grow your business significantly. What is it? I call it the *controlling idea*.

A good campaign begins and ends with a controlling idea. I first heard the term *controlling idea* when I was researching how to write a screenplay and found the idea helpful, not just in writing stories but in writing books and, well, wireframing websites. A controlling idea answers the question: What is this story about? The controlling idea for Disney's *The Lion King*, a retelling of Shakespeare's *Hamlet* in many ways, might be: a young lion must gain the confidence necessary to confront his evil uncle, who murdered his father, so that he can take his rightful place as king of the jungle and return order and life to his homeland.

After a storyteller determines their controlling idea, they *must* submit all copy to that idea if the story is going to make their point and resonate with an audience. If our controlling idea involves a lost dog returning home to his family, who realize how much they loved the previously neglected dog, we should not include too many scenes about a food critic attempting to start their own restaurant. Both, to be sure, may be entertaining stories, but when we combine plots the audience has to burn too many mental calories trying to figure out what the story is about. In short, subplots aside, a good story will support only one major plot.

Certainly a story can present multiple ideas, and those ideas are sometimes subjective, but very few stories are commercially successful if the plot is up for interpretation. Stories that have a singular focus, such as "an underdog having their day" or "good triumphing over evil", gain much more popular appeal, if for no other reason than they require less mental effort to consume and enjoy.

How the clarity of a controlling idea in a narrative relates to your brand message is simple. If I spend two minutes looking at your marketing collateral, I need to understand the main idea you are trying to communicate, and I need to be able to state it back to you clearly. For instance, one of the clients in my mastermind, Jeff Tomaszewski, owns a franchise of gyms called MaxStrength Fitness. As I reviewed Jeff's website and marketing collateral, I struggled to understand what differentiated his gym from the thousands of others in North America.

"What makes your gym different?" I asked Jeff.

"Well," he said, "What makes us different, I believe, is that our trainers work with our clients for only twenty minutes, twice each week. They focus on resistance training rather than cardio. The workouts are challenging but short. And the results are incredible."

"So this is a program for busy people who don't have the time to live at the gym?" I asked.

"Exactly," he replied.

After asking if he had a franchise in Nashville yet (because I wanted to sign up immediately), I asked why that controlling idea wasn't all over his website. In fact, the idea that a customer could get results while working out for only twenty minutes twice each week was buried well below the fold on his website, deep into the text toward the bottom of the page.

Reviewing Jeff's website reminded me how important a controlling idea is in any marketing or messaging campaign. In a messaging context, it is the one idea you want your audience to remember most, and as such your messaging collateral should be delivered like a memorization exercise. In other words, once you come up with your controlling idea, you want to repeat it so many times your audience practically memorizes it. For Jeff, the controlling idea was "You work out for twenty minutes, twice each week." This needed to be stated clearly in the header and repeated over each section of his website, in the title or subtitle of the lead generator, in every subsequent email that went out after the lead generator was downloaded, on the "about us" page, in the "a word from our CEO" video, in customer testimonials, and on and on. As far as I'm concerned, the message, shortened to "twenty minutes, twice," could be printed on hats and coffee mugs and T-shirts and banners being dragged by airplanes in the sky.

A controlling idea needs to be a complete idea, but I will let "twenty minutes, twice" slide if the thought has been explained in length enough times that people understand what the abbreviated version of it means.

HAVE YOU DEFINED A CONTROLLING IDEA?

Most small businesses have not defined their controlling idea and therefore distribute a muddled message into the marketplace. When I look at your messaging collateral, would I be able to tell what your controlling idea is or, more importantly, whether you even have one? If not, you've got an amazing opportunity to grow your business through clear messaging, marketing material, and, most importantly, word of mouth.

How do you come up with your controlling idea? You already have. If you've created a StoryBrand BrandScript, your controlling idea is staring right back at you. As you read your BrandScript, ask yourself, "What is this story really about?" or, better, "What is the moral of the story I am inviting customers into?" Is the moral "You shouldn't have to pay more for car insurance" or "Natural peanut butter shouldn't taste like cardboard"?

Whatever it is, your controlling idea is "the point" you're trying to make in all your messaging collateral.

You should have one controlling idea, and it should be stated simply. It should be easy to understand. Your BrandScript forces your story to be simple and clear. Your controlling idea should get a positive reaction from your customers (without you having to explain it at all) and should be repeated several times as a customer scrolls down the page. Remember, good messaging is an exercise in memorization, meaning you are trying to get your customer to memorize your controlling idea so they can repeat it to their friends and your business will grow. Short, simple statements repeated word for word, over and over, is an effective messaging strategy.

Your controlling idea is so important that I've added it to your StoryBrand BrandScript tool. You will see a space for it at the bottom of the BrandScript at StoryBrand.AI. Feel free to edit and refine your controlling idea as the story of your brand develops in your own mind.

If it will help, use the StoryBrand Brain at StoryBrand.AI to define and refine your controlling idea. If you take only one thing from this book, please leave with a controlling idea and use it often. If you do, you will get the money back that you paid for this book a thousand times over.

In the next section, I will guide you through a process to take your clear message and use it in all manner of marketing and messaging collateral. For now, though, take some time to determine a controlling idea for your brand. What is the main differentiator that sets you apart from your competition? What one idea would most quickly clarify your offer? What idea do you want your customers to repeat as a way of introducing your brand to others? These are the kinds of questions you want to consider as you brainstorm the controlling idea section of your BrandScript.

CLARIFY YOUR MESSAGE SO CUSTOMERS LISTEN

- Go to StoryBrand.AI and either create a BrandScript or log in to your existing BrandScript.
- Brainstorm the controlling idea sound bite for your brand. What is the moral of the story you are inviting customers into? What's the one big idea you want your StoryBrand BrandScript to communicate?
- Use the "controlling idea" line of your BrandScript to capture your new and important sound bite.

Controlling Idea ______________________________

SECTION 3

EXECUTING YOUR STORYBRAND MESSAGING AND MARKETING CAMPAIGN

CHAPTER 13

HOW TO EXECUTE A FLAWLESS STORYBRAND MESSAGING CAMPAIGN

We will see an increased engagement from customers only if we implement our StoryBrand BrandScript in a marketing and messaging campaign. The BrandScript you've put together has to show up on websites and in email campaigns, elevator pitches, and sales scripts. The sound bites you have created must be repeated over and over for years to come if you are hoping to grow your business.

The degree to which you implement your StoryBrand BrandScript into marketing and messaging material is the degree to which people will understand why they need your products and/or services and begin to place orders.

It's surprisingly easy to fool yourself into thinking that just because you clarified your message, customers can read your mind. Let's be clear: Your message is clear to you, but until you speak it and repeat it, it isn't clear to anybody else. To get results, your message must be clear in the minds of others.

This, then, is the goal of a communication campaign: If you are running for office, your job is to install your clear message into the minds of the body politic. If you are building a brand, your job is to act as though your products and services are running for office.

Years ago, I was asked to come to the headquarters of a presidential favorite. The candidate had served as governor of a large state and went into the campaign with an enormous lead and the locked-down electoral votes of his own state. He had national name recognition, had over a hundred million dollars behind his campaign, and had the support of his political party behind him. And he was failing. His campaign was shrinking in the polls month after month.

When I met with his team, I introduced them to the StoryBrand framework and emphasized why their candidate needed to repeat sound bites—sound bites that clarified what the country needed; sound bites that defined our nation's biggest problems from an external, internal, and philosophical perspective; sound bites that positioned himself as the guide and the body politic as the hero; sound bites that laid out a simple, three-step plan; sound bites that painted a clear picture of a bright future; sound bites that warned voters of the negative consequences of wasting their vote on somebody else; sound bites that offered an aspirational identity for the country; and finally a sound bite that affirmed a vote for him was the right decision.

His campaign leadership, sadly, explained that their candidate was not a "sound bite kind of guy." Instead, they told me he was a scholar. He had written books about his policy ideas. He was authentic and intelligent. He was more at home in a town hall meeting answering questions off the cuff and believed in the necessity of nuance. He wanted to be in meetings, studying the issues, devising plans to solve America's biggest problems. Honestly, the more they described their candidate, the more I thought he should be president. And the more they described him, the more I realized he would never be president. I told them so.

"You are doing everything to prepare this man to be president and nothing to get him elected," I said.

This same dynamic is likely true of you and your products and services. You did the work to create terrific products and services and are capable of delivering. But building great products and services and being able to talk about them effectively requires two separate sets of skills. The idea that "if you build it, they will come" may work to summon ghosts to a baseball field in Kansas, but it will not work to grow your business. To sell products and services, you must build them and then talk about them. And when you're done talking about them, you must talk about them again. And then again.

Having spent ten years helping brands clarify their message, I've come to believe people have to read or hear your message about eight times before they internalize and respond to that message. On top of that, people ignore most commercial messages, so you have to repeat your clear message over and over for them to hear it even once. If 90 percent of all commercial messages are ignored, for instance, you will have to repeat your message eighty times to get somebody to hear it eight times. Your clear message needs to be stated clearly in elevator pitches, passed around in conversation, repeated clearly on your website, spoken of in your lead generators, talked about in YouTube videos, printed on your swag, painted on the wall of your retail establishment, written about in emails and snail mail, and spoken from the mouths of your sales representatives. Your message should be communicated in any digital ads you create, podcast openings and closings, keynote presentations, and so on and so on. In other words, your clear message is going to require a campaign.

The third section of *Building a StoryBrand* gives both large and small companies tangible, practical steps they can take to apply their BrandScript into messaging and marketing collateral. Whether you're a mom-and-pop shop, a start-up, a personal brand, a multibillion-dollar organization, or even a presidential candidate, in the following chapters I'll show you the lessons we've learned from the thousands of companies who have effectively created and executed on their StoryBrand BrandScript to see radical results. The first step, though, is simple: talk differently.

CLARIFY AND MEMORIZE YOUR SOUND BITES

Stop rambling. When you talk about your brand, know what you are going to say long before you are asked to speak. Don't wing it. Don't make it up as you go along. You will immediately find that when you start using the sound bites you have created to talk about your brand, people pay attention.

Years ago I came up with my own BrandScript sound bites to describe StoryBrand itself. I noticed that when I repeated my sound bites, people leaned in, and, to be honest, the interest wasn't always welcome. If somebody sitting next to me on a plane asked what I did for work, I'd answer with my sound bite and then have to spend the rest of the flight looking at their website or rewriting the speech they were going to deliver to whatever audience they were flying out to address. My favorite encounter was with an Uber driver in Baltimore. He'd picked me up at the Baltimore Airport and was dropping me off at my client's headquarters only a few miles away. I knew we wouldn't be in the car long, so when he asked what I did, I decided to test the effectiveness of my sound bite: Sometimes business leaders have great ideas and great products, but they don't know how to talk about them to get people to pay attention. When they can't come up with the sound bites they need to get their ideas across, they call me. I help business leaders come up with the sound bites they need to sell more products or get more votes.

The young man driving the car turned down his stereo, thought for second, and said to me, "You are a very important person." I laughed. I guess my sound bite worked, sort of. He then explained he needed some messaging advice. I figured he had a side hustle and wanted some advice to grow his business, but it turned out something else was true: he needed messaging advice in order to break up with his girlfriend. He literally pulled his car over at the gates of a national security building where I was scheduled to meet with a client and started talking about their relationship and how she just didn't get him and that she'd been seeing this other guy. I'd suddenly been dropped into an episode of *The Bachelor.* Men with guns were watching us from behind the barricades, and so as he talked I was torn. I didn't want to get shot, but I was deeply curious about what she saw in this other guy. Anyway, I'm not a relationship counselor, but I did give him a few lines. I say I gave him messaging advice, but truthfully most of the short conversation consisted of me saying things like, "Don't say that. Definitely don't say that." To be honest, I think she might have been better off without him, but that's hardly the point. The point is, when you use your sound bites to talk about your brand, people should turn down the radio. People should pull over. They should understand exactly why you and your brand are so important.

What follows is a short, simple three-step process to get your message across in a successful communication campaign.

Step One: Create Your StoryBrand BrandScript

If you've not been creating your BrandScript as you've read this book, go back and start at the beginning. The process of creating a BrandScript will clarify your offer not only to customers but to yourself and your team. Don't think just because you know you shouldn't play the hero that your audience will start seeing you as their guide, for instance. They will see you as the guide only when you use sound bites that demonstrate you empathize with their problem and then use sound bites that demonstrate your competency to help them solve their problem. Create your StoryBrand BrandScript.

Step Two: Edit Your Sound Bites Until They Get the Reaction You Want

If you've created the right sound bites, they should stop people in their tracks. When you're done repeating your sound bites, people should ask for your business card or, better, hand you their credit card. If, on the other hand, people ask for clarification so they can understand what you were trying to say, you don't quite have your sound bites dialed in. The only question people should have after you repeat your sound bite is, How can

I buy it? In fact, if you've used your call to action sound bite, they shouldn't even be asking that question because you already answered it. In short, when you use your sound bites, people should either want to place an order or know somebody they think should place an order.

Consider your StoryBrand BrandScript a rough draft. The number one problem I've encountered in coaching people through the process is their initial sound bites are too elusive. You can't be vague if you want your sound bites to work. Remember, don't be clever; be clear.

Your StoryBrand BrandScript should be a work in progress until it succeeds. If you aren't getting the reaction you want, keep refining the sound bites until they lead to engagement and orders. This can be a difficult process for some, especially if you really like the way you've been talking about your brand. But the fact that you really like something likely has more to do with the process you and your team went through or how hard it was to come to an agreement or the fact your granddaughter came up with your tagline or the idea that your sound bite rhymes. Please, God, help us all. The only thing you should be paying attention to when it comes to creating a StoryBrand BrandScript is whether customers are leaning in and placing orders. Keep evolving your sound bites until they get the reaction you want.

Step Three: Repeat Your Sound Bites Until the Public Has Them Memorized

Think of your communication campaign as an exercise in memorization. Your job is to repeat your sound bites over and over so many times that your customers can repeat them back to you.

Around my house we don't give out an allowance. Chores exist because children are a critical part of the family, and we all have to contribute to the family objectives, which, in our home, are all about loving and respecting each other and the guests who enter our home. That said, our daughter has a terrific opportunity to make money, which is by memorizing poems. When I was young, I memorized poetry and I credit my success as a writer to this practice. Not only this, but the countless hours I spent repeating Kipling's "The God's of the Copybook Headings" or William Blake's "The Tyger" in my mind were the hours I wasn't going to the stupid places I'd likely have taken my mind. And how do you memorize something (or more accurately, help somebody else memorize something)? You help them repeat whatever it is you want them to memorize over and over in the exact same language. This is why the alphabet song is so effective. It is essentially a marketing jingle that has been helping people effectively memorize the alphabet for a century or more. If you want to memorize a poem, you carry it around on an index card and pull it out of your pocket to read it whenever you're standing in line at a coffee shop or waiting for a movie to begin.

When my wife's baby sister turned twelve, I gave her a binder filled with ten classic poems. On the back side of each poem, I taped a $100 bill in an envelope. I let her know that whenever she memorized each of the ten poems, she could have and spend the $100 associated with that poem. What did I really give her for her birthday? I gave her the transformation that takes place when a person meditates on some of the greatest words ever captured in the English language. In other words, I gave her the opportunity for personal transformation.

Your messaging campaign works like that binder, except instead of your customer getting $100 every time they memorize your sound bite, they pay you money in the form of an order.

If you want to use your StoryBrand BrandScript to grow your business, take the three steps necessary to roll out a messaging campaign: Create your BrandScript, edit your BrandScript, and then repeat your BrandScript. After that, let's start dropping your refined sound bites into effective marketing collateral.

In the next chapter we will begin putting your BrandScript to use in the form of effective marketing and messaging collateral, starting with your website.

CHAPTER 14

HOW TO GET YOUR WEBSITE RIGHT

I believe your website is important *secondly* because customers will look at it and place orders but *firstly* because, by wireframing a good website, you are organizing your talking points in such a way that *you* can better understand your offer. If you spend a week, for instance, slowly plotting out the sections of your website, making sure to get the language right, and putting that language in the right order, you are effectively clarifying how your offer is going to be spelled out to the world. These sound bites and this language will translate into conversations at cocktail parties, emails to clients, and internal talking points delivered to your own team.

There have been many instances in which I came up with a

new product idea and then sat down to wireframe the landing page for that product before I really understood my own offer. The exercise of wireframing a website is worth the trouble.

To help you wireframe your website (get the text right and put it in the right order), my team has created an artificial intelligence tool that will help you move past the blank page. After you create your StoryBrand BrandScript at StoryBrand. AI, simply press the "Create my Messaging and Marketing Campaign" button and our AI prompts will guide you through a series of questions that will inform the text on your new website. The tool is being updated consistently so that it works better and better. When you're done, you can easily hand your wireframe to a designer who can lay it out for you. If you hire a StoryBrand certified coach, they can further edit your text based on best practices from their experience. The result should be a landing page or website that gets terrific results.

Most of us don't have millions to spend on a marketing campaign, but that's okay. These days we can get serious traction just paying attention to the words we use and the places we can find to repeat those words, and all of that starts with a clear and effective website. People may hear about us through word of mouth or social media, but when they do, they often visit our website to learn more. When they get to our website, our controlling idea should be spelled out more clearly than they've ever heard it before.

In the next chapter, I will give you a step-by-step plan to create a StoryBrand Messaging and Marketing Campaign, including eight specific sections to create for your landing page, but for now here are five best practices to keep in mind when building your website.

FIVE BEST PRACTICES WHEN BUILDING YOUR WEBSITE

1. An Offer Above the Fold

When people go to your website, the first thing they see are the images and text above the fold. The term *above the fold* comes from the newspaper industry and refers to the stories printed above where the newspaper folds in half. On a website, the images and text above the fold are the things you see and read before you start scrolling down.

As I mentioned earlier, I like to think of the messages above the fold as a first date, and then as you scroll you can treat the messages further down the page as a second and third date. But as we've talked about, the stuff you share on a first date should be short, enticing, and exclusively customer-centric.

My wife was recently gifted an online membership to a cooking school in Seattle. A friend sent it to her as a thank-you for some work she'd done on their website. At first, Betsy was excited, until she went to the site. On the main page of the site (before she logged in), there was a beautiful picture of a carrot cake along with some kind of inside joke about having something to eat while watching *Game of Thrones*. We didn't get it. She scrolled down and clicked on a video, hoping it would explain what kind of thing she'd been given. Instead, the video featured a cartoon explanation of how the company got started. Somebody named Joe met somebody named Karen, who was friends with somebody named Todd, and they all loved cooking!

It wasn't until my wife signed in and began exploring what the site offered that she got excited. She came to bed that night telling me about a certain kind of natural ingredient she could use to take the color out of liquor so all her cocktails would look clear. I didn't understand why this was important until she explained that the sage from her garden would stand out more as it hung from the glass. "Oh, the sage," I said. "They offer a service to help your sage stand out."

"No," Betsy said. "It took me a couple of hours to figure it out, but the whole subscription is about these three fun friends in Seattle who are going to make me a pro in the kitchen!"

BINGO! Betsy said it. She said the very words that needed to be printed above the fold on their website:

"We Will Make You a Pro in the Kitchen!"

One short sentence (a controlling idea) would have helped us understand what the business in question offered and even given us words to use to help their business spread.

There is no telling how many customers that site is losing because they are making their customers work so hard to understand why anybody would need their service. My own wife, who now loves the site, would have bounced had she not been given a free pass.

The idea here is that customers need to know what's in it for them right when they read the text. The text should be bold and the statement should be short. It should be easy to read and not buried under buttons and clutter. I recently went to the website for Squarespace, and it simply said, "We Help You Make Beautiful Websites." Perfect. They could have said a lot of things on their website, but because they know to keep messages short and relevant, they're making hundreds of millions of dollars.

Also, make sure that above the fold, the images and text you use meet one of the following criteria:

- **THEY PROMISE AN ASPIRATIONAL IDENTITY.**

  By offering to make my wife a pro in the kitchen, the school in Seattle could have let her know "what's in it for her" by appealing to an aspirational identity. Can we help our customers become competent in something? Will they be different people after they've engaged us? Let's spell it out clearly.
- **THEY PROMISE TO SOLVE A PROBLEM.**

  If you can fix a problem, tell us. Can you stop my cat from clawing the furniture? My car from overheating? My hair from thinning? Say it. We didn't go to your website to read about how many company softball games you've won; we came here to solve a problem.
- **THEY STATE EXACTLY WHAT THEY DO.**

  The easiest thing we can do on our website is state exactly what we do. There's a shop down the street from us called Local Honey, which would cause anybody to think they sell local honey. They quickly overcame this confusion, though, with a tagline that says, "We Sell Clothes. We Do Hair." Gotcha. Local Honey sells clothes and does hair. I've now filed them away in the Rolodex of my brain and will remember them when I need a new hairstyle or new clothes.

Take a look at your website and make sure you have an obvious offer above the fold. Some of our clients make the mistake of spelling out their offer in the middle of a paragraph that starts out, "We've been in business since 1979, committed to excellence and caring about our customers . . ." That's all nice and sweet, but J. K. Rowling didn't start her first Harry Potter novel with "My name is J. K. Rowling and for a long time I've wanted to write a book . . ." The fact that she always wanted to write a book wasn't part of the actual Harry Potter story, and she was smart enough to know the difference between her story and the story her readers wanted to read. Instead, she got straight to the point. She hooked the reader. She was smart, and we can be smart too. An offer above the fold is a sure way to get a customer hooked on the story we're inviting them into.

2. Obvious Calls to Action

If you're not sure what a call to action is, go back and read chapter 8. It's important. For now, know that the whole point of your website is to create a place where the direct call to action button makes sense and is enticing. While we're in business to serve our customers and better the world, we'll be out of business soon if people don't click that "Buy Now" button. Let's not hide it.

There are two main places we want to place a direct call to action. The first is at the top right of our website, and the second is in the center of the main section that is above the fold. Your customer's eye moves quickly in a Z pattern across your website, so if the top left is your logo and perhaps tagline, your top right is a "Buy Now" button, and the middle of the page is an offer followed by another "Buy Now" button, then you've likely gotten through all the noise in your customer's mind and they know exactly what to do if they want help solving their problem.

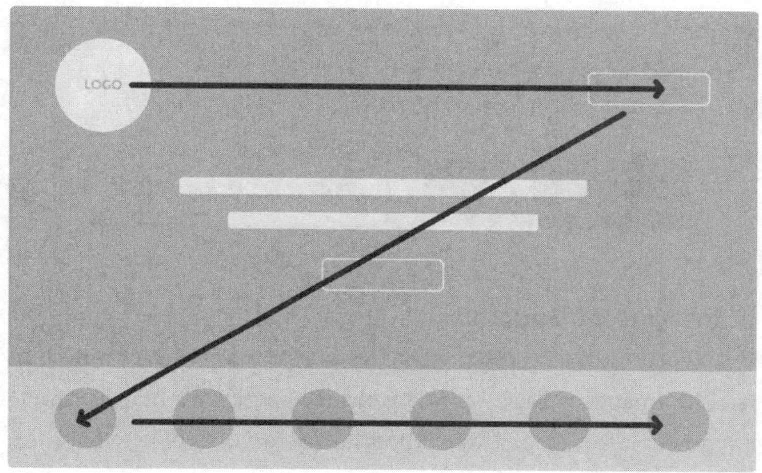

For best results the "Buy Now" buttons should be a different color from any other button on the site (preferably brighter so it stands out), and all of your "Buy Now" buttons should look exactly the same. I know this sounds like overkill, but remember, people don't read websites, they scan them. You want that button to keep showing up so nobody forgets where you want this relationship to go. A person has to hear something (or read something) many times before they process the information, so we want to repeat our main call to action over and over.

Your call to action does not need to say "buy now" specifically, but it should be a call to action that leads directly to an economic transaction. Some popular calls to action include "buy now," "schedule a call," "schedule a meeting," "get yours now," and "add to bag."

Your transitional call to action should also be obvious, but don't let it distract from the direct call to action. I like featuring the transitional call to action in a less-bright button next to the call to action so the "Will you marry me?" and "Can we go out again?" requests are right next to each other. Remember, if you aren't asking people to place an order, they won't.

BUY NOW DOWNLOAD PDF

3. Images of Success

Words make up the majority of our messaging, but not all of it. The images we use on our websites can either help communicate our offer or confuse potential customers about where the story we are inviting them into will take them. If people come to our website and see pictures of our building, we're likely wasting some of their mental bandwidth on meaningless images, unless, of course, we are trying to sell our building. But even then, images of the building aren't what I'd lead with. I'd save that for the second date. We believe images of smiling, happy people who have had a pleasurable experience (closed an open story loop) by engaging our brand should be featured on our website.

Everybody wants to experience a better life in some way or another, and while they may seem like a simple addition, images of people smiling or looking satisfied speak to us. Images have the power to show customers an emotional destination they can arrive at when they choose to place an order.

We should also display images of our products, but if we can feature those products in the hands of smiling people, our images will have more power to convert browsers into buyers. Not everybody needs to be smiling, of course; this wouldn't seem authentic. But in general we need to visually display the health, well-being, and satisfaction customers can experience with our brand. The easiest way to do this is by featuring images of happy customers.

4. A Menu of Products, All Designed to Solve One Umbrella Problem

Imagine visiting a restaurant and being told by the waiter that they don't have a menu. When you ask what your options are, they tell you, "We have really great protein and some terrific complex and simple carbohydrates." You'd sit there baffled, wondering how you are ever going to relieve your hunger. For a hundred years or more, restaurants (and for that matter most businesses) have offered their customers a menu to choose from, and your business is no different. Make sure you've listed the products people can buy from you right there on your website. And if you don't have a menu of products because you're a service-based company, then start packing your services and calling them something, thus turning those services into a product. For instance, if you sell HVAC repair, offer a product called "one-year maintenance package" that takes existing services, packages them together, and charges a price for them.

If your menu of products is complicated (for instance, if you have some B2B products and some B2C products), don't worry. A common challenge for many businesses is that they need to communicate simply about what they do, but they've diversified their revenue streams so widely that they're having trouble knowing how to frame their menu of products so that it's clear what main problem their brand solves for their customer. If this is your struggle, you're hardly alone. We had a client a couple of years ago who had two main products: a two-day personalized life-planning process for individuals, and a two-day strategic operations planning session for teams of executive leaders. Sounds simple enough, except the company didn't really make money off either product; instead, they made money training and certifying facilitators. The challenge, then, was to increase demand for each product so more people would want to become facilitators. This means they had to drive traffic to three different products: the life-planning product, the strat-ops product, and the actual money-making facilitator certification.

If this company sounds like yours (that is, your product offering is complicated), the first challenge is to find an overall umbrella message that unifies your various streams. For our friends delivering life-planning and strat-ops facilitation, we chose the need people have for a customized plan. Above the fold on their website, we recommended the text "The Key to Success Is a Customized Plan" over an image of a facilitator mapping out a plan on a whiteboard for a satisfied client. As potential customers scrolled down the page, they would see two sections to choose from: personal life plans and corporate strategy plans. Each of these buttons led to new pages with messages filtered by two different BrandScripts. Customers were able to schedule facilitations on either page. The key to growing the business, though, was a button at the top and bottom of each and every page that said, "Become a Trained Facilitator."

We may think our menu of products is too diverse to communicate our offering clearly, but it probably isn't. Certainly there are examples where various brands within an umbrella company need to be split up and marketed separately, but in most cases we can find an umbrella theme to unite them all. Once we have an umbrella message, we can separate the divisions using different web pages and different BrandScripts. The key is clarity. When we break down our divisions clearly so people can understand our overall offer followed by the menu of products that represents the various ways we can solve our customers' problems, customers will be able to choose their own adventure without being confused.

5. Very Few Words

People don't read websites anymore; they scan them. If there is a paragraph above the fold on your website, it's being passed over, I promise. Around the office we use the phrase "write it in Morse code" when we need marketing copy. By "Morse code" we mean copy that is brief, punchy, and relevant to our customers. Think again about our caveman sitting in his cave. "You sell cupcakes. Cupcakes good. Me want eat cupcake. Me like pink one and must go to bakery now." Most of us err too far in the opposite direction of simple and brief: we use too much text.

If you're promoting a school, why say, "As parents ourselves, we understand what it feels like to want the best for our children. That's why we've created a school where parents work closely with teachers through every step of their child's education journey," when you could just say, "Weekly Conference Calls with Your Child's Teacher" as a bullet point along with five other great differentiators about your school?

As customers scroll down your page, it's okay to use more words than you are using in your header, but by more I really mean a few more sentences here and there. Some of the most effective websites I've reviewed have used ten sentences or less on the entire page. That's the equivalent of about ten tweets or one press conference with Bill Belichick.

If you do want to use a long section of text to explain

something (we do it on our site, in fact), just place a little "read more" link at the end of the first or second sentence in a section of the website down the page a bit so people can expand the text if they like. That way you aren't bombarding customers with too much text.

As an experiment, let's see if you can cut half the words out of your current website. Can you replace some of your text with images? Can you reduce whole paragraphs into three or four bullet points? Can you summarize sentences into snappy sound bites? If so, make those changes soon. The rule is this: the fewer words you use, the more likely it is that people will read them.

STAY ON SCRIPT

There are more than five things to consider when building your website, of course, but if you added all the rest of the tips and strategies together, they wouldn't make as big of a difference as getting these five things right.

If you think about your StoryBrand BrandScript as a drum kit, think of your website as a drum solo. There shouldn't be a single word, image, or idea shared on your website that doesn't come from the sound bites generated by your BrandScript. The words you use in your marketing and messaging don't have to be the exact text you have on your BrandScript, but the ideas should be the same. If you're including messages on your website that don't come from one of the categories of the SB7 framework, your customers will hear only noise.

The big idea is to stay on script. People will engage your brand only after they hear, understand, and perhaps even unknowingly memorize your sound bites. If you want your words to spread, keep your sound bites short and relevant, then repeat them everywhere you can. If you do, you will engage more customers, and those customers will place more orders. Why? Not because your message is clever or even coercive but because you've finally made it clear.

When you hit the "Create a StoryBrand Messaging and Marketing Campaign" button on your StoryBrand BrandScript at StoryBrand.AI, you will be asked several questions that will inform the creation a robust report including a tagline, one-liner, wireframed website, lead generator, follow-up emails, sales script, narrative scripts for YouTube videos and social media, podcast prompts and topics, bonus ideas to create urgency, upsell product ideas, plug-and-play social media posts, plus industry trends specific to your industry. The website wireframe our artificial intelligence will create includes a few more sections than I've included in this chapter, and you can edit your wireframe so it reads exactly how you want. Your wireframe can then be easily handed to a StoryBrand certified coach to be designed and executed so that it generates (or improves) sales.

CHAPTER 15

HOW TO EXECUTE A STORYBRAND MESSAGING AND MARKETING CAMPAIGN

Transform your marketing by implementing your clear message in a marketing system that works

So where do we go from here? Now that we have a StoryBrand BrandScript, how can we use these powerful sound bites so they have the greatest possible impact on our bottom line?

The StoryBrand Messaging and Marketing Campaign is a proven, simple marketing system that works. This is basically a communication campaign you roll out so that customers hear about your brand, begin to trust that you can solve their problems, and then place orders.

We have certified nearly a thousand StoryBrand coaches in

the last ten years, each of whom understands the framework and is practiced in putting your sound bites in the right places within an effective messaging and marketing campaign. In the hundreds of meetings we've had with our coaches, they've shared with us what works and what doesn't. This chapter is a summation of their most effective practices. You can either create your messaging and marketing campaign on your own or hire a coach to create some or all of your campaign from our Coach directory at MarketingMadeSimple.com. What follows is a step-by-step execution plan. Again, much of your rough draft can be done using the StoryBrand Brain at StoryBrand.AI, but refining your work, designing your messaging and marketing campaign, and hooking it up to a CRM can all be done either by yourself or by one of our coaches.

YOUR STEP-BY-STEP PLAN

Every step you take should result in greater customer engagement and more sales. You don't have to create your entire messaging and marketing campaign all at once. That said, the more you create, the more customers will encounter and understand your offer.

Also, once you're done creating your StoryBrand Messaging and Marketing Campaign, create another one. My business has a dozen or more messaging and marketing campaigns operating, and each of them brings in leads that help us sell various products, from certifications to workshops to masterminds and private strategy sessions. Every morning I open my dashboard to see how many leads came in for each product, and I can follow those leads down a pipeline to see how many are converting to sales. In other words, I'm able to predict revenue long before a customer purchases our products, which is helpful knowledge to have when trying to grow a small business. I want the same for you.

If you are going to create your messaging and marketing campaigns plan yourself, what follows can serve as your complete roadmap. If you have a marketing director on your team, simply hand them this book and give them the task of completing the BrandScript assignment (the previous chapters in this book) and the StoryBrand Messaging and Marketing Campaign 1 that makes up this final chapter.

The reason a StoryBrand Messaging and Marketing Campaign works so well is because it guides customers through the three stages of relationships: curiosity, enlightenment, and commitment.

When a potential customer hears your elevator pitch, they get curious. The reason they get curious is because they suspect you have a product or service that can help them. It's only when a customer gets curious that they want to know more, so the first job of a good messaging and marketing campaign is to make them curious. After a customer gets curious, they begin to read a little more about your product to "enlighten" themselves about whether your product is right for them. In this enlightenment stage, depending on how expensive or complicated the product adoption might be, a customer may look around for reviews, read about your product, ask their friends if they've used the product, or search YouTube for videos about your product. If you have good "enlightenment" material, customers will then move on to the third phase of their relationship with you, and that is the "commitment" phase in which they become willing to place an order.

Our goal as marketers is to create terrific curiosity collateral—that is, sound bites on landing pages and digital ads and webinars and the like that will pique a potential customer's curiosity. After we create our curiosity collateral, we need to create enlightenment collateral, which may include downloadable PDFs, webinars, breakout session presentations, automated email sequences, YouTube videos, and other long-form marketing collateral. Once we've created our enlightenment collateral, we need to make sure our calls to action are clear, including sales emails, countdown timers, special offers, and so on.

The job of a messaging and marketing campaign is to pique our customers' curiosity; earn their trust with consistent, valuable information; and then ask for the commitment by challenging them to make a purchase. If you follow the step-by-step instructions in this chapter, your StoryBrand Messaging and Marketing Campaign will do the job perfectly.

With that, let's get started with the first step.

STEP ONE: GENERATE A STORYBRAND BRANDSCRIPT

It goes without saying that your StoryBrand BrandScript is the foundation of your messaging and marketing campaign. Until you get the words right, your marketing will fail. To get the best results, create a BrandScript for every major marketing initiative. You can do this by reading this book, listening to the audiobook, or, if you want to have a little fun, listen to *StoryBrand Radio Theater Presents: Pete and Joe Save Their Mother's Company* on Audible or Youtube.com/@storybrand. The radio theater version of *Building a StoryBrand* is a fictional story that teaches the framework, followed by me explaining a step-by-step process you can go through to create a BrandScript. The radio theater version of *Building a StoryBrand* was designed to be a quick and effective way for you (or your team) to understand and create a BrandScript.

Once you've created your BrandScript, move on to step two.

STEP TWO: CREATE A ONE-LINER

Most people turn customers off the second they start talking about their business. When somebody asks what we do and we answer with something like, "Well, it's complicated" or "You see, fifty years ago my grandfather started our company . . ." we've lost the customer's interest immediately. Instead of rambling, though, imagine memorizing a single statement you could recite to intrigue and even engage a potential customer. Imagine this statement being so powerful it causes people to ask for your business card or, better, inquire about how they could place an order.

A one-liner is a better way to answer the question, "What do you do?" It's more than a slogan or tagline; it's a single statement that helps people realize why they need your products or services.

To understand how it works, let's take another page out of the storyteller's playbook. When screenwriters pitch their screenplays to studio executives, the difference between being accepted or rejected often comes down to what's called a *logline*.

A logline is simply a movie's one-sentence description. A strong logline will help the screenwriter sell the screenplay and will continue to be used all the way through a movie's opening weekend so that promoters can sell it to moviegoing audiences. If you've ever scrolled through a movie app on your phone or scrolled through Netflix looking for something to watch, chances are you've read a logline. Here are a few examples:

> "A precocious private high school student whose life revolves around his school competes with its most famous and successful alumnus for the affection of a first-grade teacher."
>
> —*Rushmore*

> "Blacksmith Will Turner teams up with eccentric pirate 'Captain' Jack Sparrow to save his love, the governor's daughter, from Jack's former pirate allies, who are now undead."
>
> —*Pirates of the Caribbean: The Curse of the Black Pearl*

> "A science-fiction fantasy about a naive but ambitious farm boy from a backwater desert who discovers powers he never knew he had when he teams up with a feisty princess, a mercenary space pilot, and an old wizard warrior to lead a ragtag rebellion against the sinister forces of the evil Galactic Empire."
>
> —*Star Wars: A New Hope*

> "An incompetent, immature, and dimwitted heir to an auto-parts factory must save the business to keep it out of the hands of his new con-artist relatives."
>
> —*Tommy Boy*

What makes these loglines complete and effective? Two things: clarity and promise. A logline is designed to summarize the story in a way that a reader understands the plot (and thus the entertainment value of the story) and desires to know more. In other words, the reader of the logline clearly understands what the movie is about and believes the promise that it will provide entertainment or inspiration.

The one-liner you will create for your company will work like a logline for a movie: it will clearly communicate your offer and promise a solution to your customer's problem. And, not unlike a logline, your one-liner will make people want to buy your product. Not only this, but your one-liner can be used to convert your entire team into a sales force. Whether it's your customer service reps, your assembly-line team, or your company's president, every member of your team should know your one-liner so that if anybody asks them about the business, they can describe it in such a way that customers clearly understand why they need your products and services.

What would life look like if everybody you worked with were converted into a salesforce spreading the word about your products and services? Creating a one-liner and having everybody repeat it over and over is a great way to spread word about the value of your products and services.

To craft a compelling one-liner, we'll employ a sound bite that comes from a distilled version of the StoryBrand framework. While a StoryBrand BrandScript has seven parts, a one-liner has three parts: the problem, the product as solution, and the result.

Your one-liner doesn't have to be a single sentence, nor does it need to be four sentences. Think of it more as a statement. You simply want to communicate these four ideas: Who is your customer? What is their problem? What is your plan to help them? What will their life look like after you do?

Let's take a deeper look at each of the three necessary components:

As I said earlier in the book, stories become interesting when the hero wants something and encounters conflict in their journey to get what they want, so if we want to get people interested in our brand, we should open our remarks by identifying our customer's conflict. For example, which of these statements makes the product sound more interesting?

Option one: Our new toothpaste is gentle on teeth and gums.
Option two: Many people have sensitive teeth and gums and experience pain when brushing their teeth. Our new toothpaste is gentle on teeth and gums.

The second option starts with the problem and then positions the product as the solution to the problem. Most people, and certainly most people who have this problem, would find the second sound bite much more intriguing. The point: the problem is the hook.

Starting your one-liner with the problem that is bothering your customer will trigger the mental response we are looking for. When we start with the problem, the customer thinks to themselves: *Yeah, I do struggle with that. Tell me more.*

HERE ARE SOME EXAMPLES OF PROBLEMS DIFFERENT BRANDS CAN TALK ABOUT:

If you're a busy mom and can't find time to work out, then . . .

If your dog barks loudly whenever somebody knocks on the door, then . . .
If you want the benefits of an electric vehicle but worry about range, then . . .

After you state the problem your customers experience, your customers will lean in. Next, we want to position our product, service, or idea as the solution to the problem, thus offering a resolution to the story loop we just opened by talking about the problem.

Now that we've clearly stated the problem, let's position our product as the solution. This should be a very, very simple addition to the one-liner. Simply state: "That's why we created X" and stop talking. When creating a one-liner, clients will often ramble on and on about their product, about its features and benefits and so on. This is a mistake. When you simply state the name or short description of the product, you resolve the open story loop and satisfy the customer's curiosity, but when you ramble on and on, you actually dilute the value of your product. For example, compare: "Many people find it difficult to fall asleep at night because they are stressed. Our meditation is based on science and over twenty years of research, relieving the central nervous system by triggering natural calming agents that are released through breath work, mental focus and . . ." with this statement: "Many people find it difficult to fall asleep at night because they are stressed. Our simple meditation helps you fall asleep fast."

Certainly the first statement is interesting, but it also wanders into the weeds. That's fine if your customer is ready to be enlightened, but enlightening your customer isn't the job of the one-liner. The one-liner's purpose is to pique curiosity so that people will want to either buy your product or seek enlightenment about why they should buy it. Your one-liner will be more effective if you keep the "product as solution" portion as short as possible.

The third and final sound bite you want to include in your one-liner is the result your customer will experience if they buy your product. Use this portion of your one-liner to cast a vision for your customer's future, thus giving them a picture of the life they could have once their problem is resolved. Human beings move toward a positive vision of their future, but only if that vision is described clearly. For example: "More and more people want to know where their beef comes from because industrialized ranching practices can leave toxins in our food, often triggering food allergies. Regenerative ranching practices ensure animals are toxin-free, which means *you don't struggle with food allergies and feel much better over time.*"

Keep Editing Your One-Liner Until It Works

Consider your first one-liner a rough draft. Write it down and test it repeatedly. Run it by your friends, spouse, potential customers, even strangers standing in line at Starbucks. Do people look interested? Do they completely understand what you offer? If so, you're on the right track. When they start asking for your business card or for more information, you've really dialed it in.

STEP THREE: WIREFRAME AN EFFECTIVE LANDING PAGE

As I mentioned in the last chapter, your website or landing page should be the best and clearest version of your sales pitch. To achieve that, use each section of your landing page to invite customers further and further into a story that piques their curiosity, enlightens them, and challenges them to make a commitment.

Of the tens of thousands of websites our StoryBrand certified coaches have created for their clients, these are the sections of a website or landing page that have proven to be the most effective.

If you have an e-commerce site selling dozens or hundreds of products, use these sections to explain your overall brand. You can then create a landing page like this for each of your individual products or services.

THE HEADER

The header is the part of your website that sits "above the fold," meaning at the top of the page. The job of the header is to explain your offer so clearly and in such simple language that your customer wants to know more. If you've used the right text, your customer will want to keep scrolling to "enlighten themselves" about all that you offer.

A good header will include a large-text offer, a transitional call to action, a direct call to action, and, if you like, a value stack (a few additional bullet points that build on your initial offer). Here is an example:

THE STAKES

The stakes section of your website is where you put the negative consequences of not doing business with you. We like this section near the top because, as you remember, the problem is the hook. Your stakes section can be developed as a paragraph, images, bullet points, or even a video. Here is a simple example:

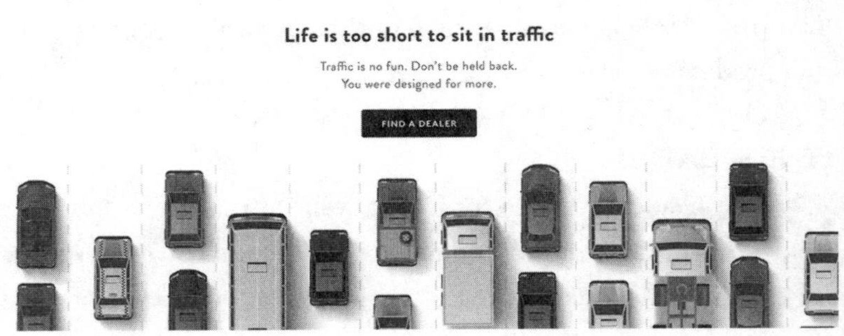

THE VALUE PROPOSITION

Since you went negative at the top, let's quickly swing back to positive. Humans love it when a story swings back and forth between happy and hard moments, so employ that technique here. In this section, you'll use a paragraph or some bullet points or even a testimonial to reiterate the value you can offer a customer. In a way, this section will be a wordier version of the header, meaning it's a slightly more elaborated version of your offer. Here's an example:

GUIDE

Now that you've invited customers into a story, introduce yourself. After all, at this point, you've likely earned the right to be heard. In this section, you want to position yourself or your brand as the guide the hero needs in order to solve their problem and win the day. Remember, in this section you want to communicate empathy and demonstrate competency. Here is an example:

THE PLAN

At this point in looking at your landing page, many customers will want to place an order, but they aren't going to. The reason? Cognitive dissonance. Something still feels confusing to them. Mostly, they wonder how the process is going to work or exactly how they will make this change in their lives. Rather than sending them away to "think about it," let's give them a three-step plan. Here is an example:

THE EXPLANATORY PARAGRAPH

Customers often want to do due diligence before placing an order, especially if you're selling something complicated or expensive. Giving your customers a few paragraphs to read about your product or service, though, allows them to spend a little time reflecting on your offer. We call this the *explanatory paragraph*, and it can look like this:

LEAD GENERATOR AD

You definitely want to share your lead generator in a pop-up ad of some sort, but you can also repeat it in the actual body of the landing page. Mentioning your lead generator twice will actually encourage even greater sign-ups. Here's a good one:

THE JUNK DRAWER

I used to joke that the junk drawer is the most important section of your website because it's where you are going to put everything you previously thought was important. Don't bother cluttering up your sales page with all kinds of links and background information about your brand. Instead, put that stuff down here at the bottom of the page.

You can add or subtract from this wireframe if you like. Regardless, using the StoryBrand Brain at StoryBrand.AI to generate a sample landing page for your brand will help you see a terrific, visual "sales pitch" for your offering. Have fun creating yours!

STEP FOUR: CREATE A LEAD GENERATOR THAT COLLECTS EMAIL ADDRESSES AND PHONE NUMBERS

There is no question people are addicted to their phones. It's a sad reality but a reality all the same. We are all staring at our phones all the time. Why? Not just because developers are making their apps more and more addictive but also because it's our primary communication device. If you are like me, you likely interact with ten or twenty times as many people through your phone in a given day as you do in person. In fact, if you send me a text message, you are communicating with me in the same medium as my family and closest friends. And, more often than not, I've invited you to do so.

If I give you my phone number for text updates, or my email address so that I can be notified about special offers, I've literally told you to reach out to me because I like your brand that much.

Brands that reach out to their customers via text and email have a strategic advantage over those who do not, mainly because brands that do so are less likely to be forgotten.

The challenge is convincing customers to give us their contact information. So how do we get people to join our email list or give us that valuable information? We offer them something in return, something more valuable than the vague offer of a newsletter or an invitation to "stay in touch." This "something" is a lead generator, a resource that magnetically attracts people to our businesses and invites them to take action. In the StoryBrand framework, we call this a *transitional call to action*. A transitional call to action, if you remember, is like asking potential customers out on a date. We're not asking them to commit to marriage, but we are asking them to spend a little more time with us.

How to Create an Irresistible Lead Generator

In order to combat noise in today's marketplace, your lead generator must do two things:

1. Provide enormous value for your customer
2. Establish you as an authority in your field

As I mentioned before, in the year we started StoryBrand, our first lead generator was a simple, downloadable document (in PDF format) called "5 Things Your Website Should Include." It was remarkably successful. More than forty thousand people downloaded it, which allowed me to email reminders about our upcoming StoryBrand Marketing Workshops. I credit that single lead generator with taking our company past the $2 million mark. From there, we created a free video series called The 5-Minute Marketing Makeover (5MinuteMarketingMakeover.com), which took our lead generation to another level. We were no longer grinding to create business. Now we create lead generators for each revenue stream our company offers. This allows us to segment our customers by their interests and offer different products to solve their various problems.

There are endless options for creating lead generators. Our StoryBrand coaches have been incredibly creative at producing lead generators that offer valuable information in exchange for an email address. Of all the lead generators our coaches have created for clients, there are five kinds that are the most effective.

Five Types of Lead Generators for All Types of Businesses

1. **Downloadable guide:** This is a shockingly inexpensive way to generate leads, and it's what we used when launching StoryBrand. Get specific. If you're a local market selling produce, offer monthly recipes or tips for tending a garden.
2. **Online course or webinar:** Creating a brief online course or webinar is involved, but it's also easier than ever. If you're an expert on something and want to position

yourself as such in the marketplace, offer a free training online in exchange for an email address. By doing so, you'll have positioned yourself as an expert, created reciprocity, and earned your customer's trust.

3. **Software demos or a free trial:** This has worked wonders for many businesses. Remember in the early nineties when AOL sent demo CDs in the mail with one thousand hours of free internet browsing for forty-five days? They worked like a charm. The internet has changed since then, but the marketing principle remains the same.
4. **Free samples:** My wife, Betsy, orders ready-to-cook meals from a business called Blue Apron. To generate more leads, Blue Apron credits her with "free sample meals" she can send to friends and family. A number of them try it, and they end up buyers.
5. **Live events:** If you've ever walked into a large pet store like Petco, you've likely seen invitations to free dog obedience classes. Even if you're a smaller operation, hosting a quarterly class is a terrific way to build a small database of qualified customers.

Still Stuck? Swipe Ideas from These Examples

One key to having an effective lead generator is giving it an irresistible title. These are some sample lead generators I've seen that worked well. There's no need to reinvent the wheel. Leverage these proven examples and create something similar.

"Five Mistakes People Make with Their First Million Dollars"
—A downloadable PDF guide offered by a financial

adviser who wanted to find young, newly wealthy clients and help them with their financial planning.

"Building Your Dream Home: Ten Things to Get Right Before You Build" —A free e-book offered by an architect who wanted to establish herself as a guide to families looking to build a custom home.

"Cocktail Club: Learn to Make One New Cocktail Each Month" —This was a monthly event surprisingly put on by a garden store that taught attendees how to infuse bitters and simple syrups with herbs. The objective for this promotion was to create a community around their store. Business is booming (or should I say blooming) because people want to attend their classes.

"Become a Professional Speaker" —A free online course offered by a speaking coach for those who wanted to become professional speakers. This generated leads for long-term subscriptions to his coaching service.

The ideas go on and on. Now that you're aware of how lead generators work and which ones work best, you'll see them everywhere. Keep a running list of lead generator possibilities. If one strikes you as exceptionally strong, get to work and create a version of your own. The key here is to avoid falling into "paralysis by analysis." The best and easiest place to start is with a downloadable PDF guide. If you aren't a writer, don't worry. There are plenty of writers for hire, and you can find some terrific StoryBrand certified coaches through our directory at MarketingMadeSimple.com.

You can also use the StoryBrand Brain at StoryBrand.AI. When you use the tool you will be given a list of possible lead generator titles and the copy you can use in the lead generator itself.

STEP FIVE: CREATE AN AUTOMATED EMAIL OR TEXT DRIP CAMPAIGN

In my mid-twenties, after traveling around the country for about a year in a Volkswagen van, I got a warehouse job at a publishing company outside Portland, Oregon. The job came to me by accident. A friend's dad owned the company and knew I needed a job. But I'm grateful. Working in publishing, even in an entry-level position, helped me fall in love with the process of making and selling books and, later, writing them myself.

Within a few years of getting that job, I was put in charge of the company. It was an unintentional move on the owner's part because other employees retired or took other jobs, and the owner kept "temporarily" moving me up. One season, though, the owner hired a consultant to help him figure out how to grow the business, and after studying the numbers, the consultant pointed at me and said, "Put that guy on commission and let him do what he wants." I was just as taken aback as my boss. Without any of us realizing it, the company had actually started growing while I was at the helm. And when we sat down and looked closely at the numbers, we realized the reason. I assure you, it had little to do with my competence at the time.

Just before my series of promotions, I'd discovered a piece of software called FileMaker Pro. We used this software to manage our database and collect orders. Every day I'd show up at the office and fiddle with the software, and one day I realized we could use it to see who had placed the largest orders and automate the creation of a mailing list and subsequent thank-you letters. This is all standard marketing these days, but back then it was relatively new technology. Each month I sent about two hundred letters to the businesses that ordered the most copies of our books. That simple gesture generated a great deal of trust and differentiated us from other publishers, which, according to our consultant, generated a great deal more business.

Honestly, the letters I wrote to our customers weren't very good. One of the letters was about a camping trip I'd taken as a kid! Shakespearean prose, this was not.

These days my letters get a lot bigger response, but looking back, even those terrible letters worked to grow our business. In fact, I doubt many of our customers even read those letters.

So why did the company grow if people weren't even reading my letters?

What I realized, in hindsight, was that every month our top customers were being reminded that we existed. Every time one of those customers saw a letter and threw it away, even without opening it, our logo was flashing across their eyes.

Content is important, but the point is, there is great power in simply reminding your customers you exist. I was young and dumb at the time, but I'd stumbled onto something. Your customers may not need your product today, and they might not need it tomorrow, but on the day they do need it, you want to make sure they remember who you are, what you offer, and where they can reach you if they want to buy it.

Send Potential Customers Regular, Valuable Emails

The days of direct mail aren't completely dead, but it goes without saying that email and text messages have largely taken over. And for good reason. My company would not be where it is without having built a large email list. Because we have collected emails, we are able to earn trust by offering free value, invite customers to helpful webinars and live streams, give away massive amounts of content, offer the free use of our software tools, and, of course, let customers know when I release a new book or product.

Now that you've obtained email addresses through your lead generator, the next step is to create an automated email campaign that provides value and earns trust.

Also, an automated email campaign is a terrific way to remind customers you exist. And if they happen to open your email (you'll be surprised at how many people actually do), then it's a great way to invite them into a story in which the value you provide can change their lives.

What is an automated email campaign? An automated email campaign is a prewritten sequence of emails that begin to go out once a person is added to your list. Some people call this an "auto-responder series," but the idea is to invite customers into a narrative that enlightens them and builds a relationship.

The same trust-building experience can be created via text too. With text, you want to keep things short and likely provide links to helpful tools, or you can limit it to sales announcements or special offers. Text, by the way, is also an incredibly effective way to keep your brand in people's minds, long before and long after they place an order. In fact, I get routine text messages from a brand called Hank's Belts. Hank sells, you guessed it, belts. I've never been much of a belt guy, but when I bought a belt from Hank's Belts as a Christmas present for my father-in-law, the business texted me almost every day for months. Surprisingly, the text messages never bothered me. They were usually special offers or announcements of a new belt or line of belts, and, well, I was kind of interested. Later, when I actually needed a new, black, dress belt, I immediately thought of Hank's Belts and visited their site and placed an order. Not only this, but I've told friends about Hank's Belts. You might think I have told friends about Hank's Belts because they make good belts, but the truth is, that's not the reason at all. Lots of companies make good belts. I told my friends about Hank's Belts because they've moved into the mental real estate of my mind by sending frequent text messages! In other words, they *made* me remember them by staying in touch and reminding me they exist. This, in short, speaks to the power of email and text-message marketing.

DOES ANYBODY READ THESE THINGS?

Don't worry if the open rates on your emails are low. A 20 percent open rate is the industry standard, so anything above that is performing well. And remember, even if a person sees and deletes an email, the goal has been accomplished: you are "branding" yourself into their universe.

If someone unsubscribes from your list, that's a good thing. That person probably never would have bought from you anyway; besides, the subtraction of an email reduces the size of your list, so you aren't paying your email service provider for emails that customer doesn't want. The last thing you want to do in your marketing is bother someone, so if a person unsubscribes, all the better. It's more important to have a list of qualified, interested subscribers than a large number of people who never intend to place an order.

I'm subscribed to plenty of mailing lists and hardly ever open emails from them. Why don't I unsubscribe? Because every twenty or so emails, they send something I actually want to open. But even the emails I don't open are effectively branding the name of those companies into my conscious mind and thus my mental list of options when it finally occurs to me that I need the sort of products they sell.

Getting Started with Email and Text Marketing

I will talk about text-message marketing in a bit. First, though, let's talk about email marketing campaigns and how they can help you grow your business. While there are many kinds of automated email campaigns, the one we recommend starting with is the *nurture campaign*. A nurture campaign is a simple email that offers your subscribers valuable information as it relates to your products or services.

Not unlike your lead generator, you want these emails to continue positioning you as the guide and to create trust and reciprocity with potential customers. There will come a time to ask for a sale, but this isn't the primary goal of a nurture campaign. A typical nurture campaign may have an email going out once each week, and the order might look like this:

Email #1: Nurture email
Email #2: Nurture email
Email #3: Nurture email
Email #4: Sales email with a call to action

The pattern of sending three nurture emails followed by a sales email can be repeated month after month for as long as you want to send them. Some brands never stop, just sending out an indefinite number of emails for as long as the customer stays subscribed to the list. I think this is smart marketing, honestly, because you never know when your customer is going to have the problem your product solves. And when they do, you want them to remember you. That said, I recommend creating a few months' worth of material to get started and then adding to that campaign as you have time to create more. The idea behind a nurture campaign is to offer something of great value and then occasionally ask for an order. If your lead generator does its job of acquiring new contacts, in a short time you will have hundreds of potential customers being introduced to and reminded of your business week after week. And when those customers need help in your area of expertise, they will remember you and place an order.

So what's the difference between a nurture email and a sales email with an offer and call to action?

What Is a Nurture Email?

A good way to craft each nurture email is to use an effective formula that offers simple, helpful advice to a customer. I've been using this formula for years because it helps me offer clear value.

Paragraph #1: Talk about a problem.
Paragraph #2: Offer a plan, idea, recipe, or formula that solves the problem.
Paragraph #3: Describe what life can look like if the problem is solved.

Paragraph #4: If possible, turn the advice into a three-step plan and use those steps to summarize your advice.

I also recommend including a postscript, aka the PS. Often, the PS is the only part of the text somebody who opens a mass email will actually read.

That's really it. If you cover these four areas as efficiently as possible, you'll be crafting emails your customers open, read, and remember. And don't forget, StoryBrand.AI can actually write a rough draft of these emails for you.

WHAT ARE THE ELEMENTS OF A GOOD NURTURE EMAIL?

Here's how a nurture email campaign works: Recently we consulted with the owner of a dog boarding company interested in growing her business. We recommended she create a lead-generating PDF called "5 Things Your Dog Thinks About When You're Away" in exchange for the email addresses of qualified customers. What dog lover wouldn't want to read a PDF with a title like that? Perfect.

A few days after somebody downloaded the PDF, they would get the first email in the nurture campaign. That email looked like this:

Subject: Should We Free Feed Our Dogs?

Dear ________,

At Crest Hill Boarding we're often asked whether it's okay to free feed our dogs. Free feeding a dog is certainly the easiest way to make sure a dog always has food and never goes hungry, but there are some problems you should know about when it comes to free feeding. Dogs that are free fed often gain excess fat later in life and other health problems can occur without our noticing.

We recommend feeding your dog a set amount, once or twice per day. After twenty minutes, if your pet hasn't eaten their food, we recommend discarding the excess and waiting until the next set time to feed them again.

By sticking to a set amount of food and a set feeding schedule, you'll be able to monitor what your dog eats and also be able to diagnose any illness your pet may be suffering from that is making them lose their appetite. This will ensure your dog stays healthy and happy long into their life.

Here's to enjoying our pets for a long, long time.

Sincerely,

X

PS. As for how much each dog should be fed, it really depends on how old your dog is and how big. Next time you and your dog are in the shop, introduce us to your dog and we'll tell you everything we know about the breed.

The bottom of this email contained our client's logo, their one-liner, and a phone number in case anyone was ready to place an order. Still, getting an order wasn't the primary concern. The primary concern was to offer something of value, position the business as the guide, create reciprocity, and, most importantly, stay familiar to the customer.

You can see how getting a weekly email like this would make our client's kennel stand out in any dog owner's mind. The next time a potential customer had to suddenly leave town, they'd fondly remember her kennel and take their dog in for boarding.

After three more emails like this, our client included an email that contained an offer and a call to action.

How to Write the Offer and Call-to-Action Email

About every third or fourth email in a nurture campaign should offer a product or service the customer can buy. The key here is to be direct. Making a passive offer is only going to make you look weak, so know going into it that your sales email is just that—an email that sells something.

THE SALES FORMULA WE PREFER LOOKS LIKE THIS:

Paragraph #1: Talk about the customer's problem.
Paragraph #2: Describe a product you offer that solves this problem.
Paragraph #3: Describe what life can look like for the reader once the problem is solved.
Paragraph #4: Ensure that purchasing your product is the right decision if they want to solve their problem, let them know how much it costs, mention any special discounts or bonuses, and then ask the customer to place an order.

A GOOD OFFER AND CALL-TO-ACTION EMAIL

Similar to the nurture email, the offer and call-to-action email aims to solve a problem. The only difference is that the solution to the problem *is* your product and a strong call to action has been inserted. You are inviting this customer to do business with you. Here's an offer and call-to-action email we wrote for Crest Hill dog kennel:

> Subject: A solution for scary boarding
>
> Dear ________,
>
> If you're anything like us, you hate leaving your dog behind when you go out of town. And you hate the idea of your dog being locked in a crate next to a bunch of other stress-inducing, barking dogs. As dog lovers, we used to hate that feeling too, and that's why we created Crest Hill Boarding.
>
> At Crest Hill, your dog plays so hard all day, they are eager to lie down at night. We have three full-time staff members throwing tennis balls and enticing dogs to run and play so they're far too distracted to realize they're anywhere other than in paradise. This means that by the end of the day all the other dogs are eager to sleep too, and so your dog rests comfortably in a mostly quiet environment. You won't believe how quiet our kennels are once we put the dogs to bed at 8 p.m.
>
> Right now you can book three nights at Crest Hill at half price. This is a onetime offer, and it's meant to introduce you to how differently we take care of your pet. We think once you see how eager your dog will be to join us, you'll feel better when you have to leave town. No more guilt. No more sad goodbyes.
>
> To take advantage of this offer, just call us. You don't even have to know when the next time you're going to leave

town. We will just mark you in our system as having taken advantage of the offer.

Call us today at 555-5555.

We can't wait for your dog to experience the Crest Hill difference.

Sincerely,
X

PS: Make sure to call today. The call will only take a couple of minutes, and you'll be in our system forever. After you call, your dog's favorite home away from home will be waiting whenever you're in need of a safe, reliable, and fun-for-your-dog solution.

This email weaves in a tremendous amount of content from Crest Hill's StoryBrand BrandScript, including the external problem and internal problem along with sound bites from the success element. The gist of the email is that if a subscriber purchases Crest Hill's offer, one of their concerns will be resolved.

Note that the call to action is strong and contains a degree of scarcity: it is a onetime offer. Anyone who reads this email knows exactly what we want them to do: call and secure a discount so they can later board their dog at Crest Hill.

What Software Should We Use?

There are many software options when it comes to creating an automated email campaign. If you're working with a designer or advertising agency, this is likely a question for them. You want your designer to work with whatever software they're accustomed to using. We are big fans of Keap because the CRM is designed for businesses that have between one and twenty-five thousand email subscribers, which covers the needs of the majority of small- to medium-size businesses. Keap also consulted with us to help build our artificial intelligence tools, and they know what they're talking about.

Start Small

Getting an email campaign up and running can feel intimidating, but the process of creating and using a CRM doesn't have to be a fearful experience. Start small. To get started, simply open a Word document and start crafting your emails or, better, use StoryBrand.AI to craft rough draft emails and then edit them to your liking. You can paste these drafts into an email or CRM later. Writing that initial email is the first step. Once you read it back to yourself, you're going to want to send it to customers. That's the beginning. When you start automating that email, you're going to start getting results, which is going to make you want to write more of them. Before you know it, you'll have a robust campaign of emails that will engage customers at all hours of the day, even while you sleep.

STEP SIX: COLLECT AND TELL STORIES OF TRANSFORMATION

As we learned earlier in the book, few things are more foundational to a compelling story than a hero's transformation. Why? Because transformation is a core desire for every human being. That's why so many stories are about the hero transforming into a better version of themselves and specifically into a person who is competent to defeat the villain and solve their problem.

People love movies about characters who transform, and they love businesses that help them experience transformation too. One of the best ways we can demonstrate how we help our customers transform is through testimonials.

Great testimonials give future customers the gift of going second. The challenge lies in getting the right kind of testimonial: one that showcases your value (the results you get for customers) and the experience people had working with you. Simply asking for a testimonial usually won't work because customers will share their feelings about you by default. "Nancy is a great friend! We highly recommend Nancy and her team!"

While those are nice words, they do very little in telling their story of transformation. In a testimonial like that, there are no specific results mentioned or details about what life is like now that the transformation has taken place.

If you're asking customers to write a testimonial for you, it's likely they are (1) too busy to give deep thought to writing the testimonial or (2) subpar writers or communicators.

Weaving together a compelling tale of transformation means you have to ask the right questions—you need some raw materials to work with. The following questions will allow you to build a bank of compelling testimonials that work with nearly any customer quickly and easily.

These questions work because they "lead" the client down a specific train of thought. Simply use these questions to create a form customers can fill out. Once they complete the form, the natural flow of the sentences will allow you to copy and paste the answers to build a client case study.

These same questions can also be used to create video testimonials. Simply invite customers to be interviewed and ask them the following questions. Once the video is edited and B-roll is inserted, you can feature your video on your website or in a sales or nurture email campaign or on a landing page.

Here are five questions most likely to generate the best response for a customer testimonial:

1. What was the problem you were having before you discovered our product?
2. What did the frustration feel like as you tried to solve that problem?
3. What was different about our product?
4. Take us to the moment when you realized our product was actually working to solve your problem.
5. Tell us what life looks like now that your problem is solved or being solved.

You can see the arc of the questions naturally yields a transformation story. Once you capture the testimonial, feature it everywhere: emails, promo videos, keynote speeches, live interviews, or at events. One season we closed each episode of the *Building a StoryBrand* podcast with an interview with someone who transformed their business and their life by applying the StoryBrand framework. The response was overwhelming. We noted an immediate uptick in book purchases and interest in becoming a StoryBrand Certified Guide.

The point is that people are drawn to transformation. When they see transformation in others, they want it for themselves. The more we feature the transformation journey our customers have experienced, the faster our business will grow.

STEP SEVEN: CREATE A SYSTEM THAT GENERATES REFERRALS

If you ask any business owner how they get new customers, the majority will say "word of mouth." It would seem obvious, then, that every business out there has a system for generating more word-of-mouth referrals. Unfortunately, that's seldom the case.

Once you create a system that funnels potential customers into becoming actual customers, the final step is to turn around and invite happy customers to become evangelists for your brand. This will happen only if you create a system that invites and incentivizes people to spread the word. Various studies conducted by the American Marketing Association have shown that referrals and peer recommendations are up to 2.5 times more responsive than any other marketing channel. A marketing effort with a 250 percent increase in efficacy means we're talking about something to take seriously.

If you've done the simple, fun work of creating your StoryBrand BrandScript, your message should be clear. When you create a process that encourages referrals, you get more and more people repeating that message to their friends and family.

Let's take a step-by-step look at what it takes to create an effective referral system.

Identify Your Existing, Ideal Customers

At the top of the current Domino's Pizza website there's a link that says, "Don't have a pizza profile? Create one." That link, even though it's in small print, is likely a huge moneymaker. Those who frequently order from the restaurant chain use this link to build their perfect pizza and then enter their credit card information to order it. Domino's then sends them occasional prompts to reorder, especially before big events like football games or holiday weekends when they know their customers are more likely to enjoy their product.

Now imagine taking that strategy to the next level. What if creating a special database of existing, passionate customers and communicating with them differently could help you generate referrals? Developing a simple campaign using tools your existing fans can use to spread word about your brand is possible. Not only could you increase your existing business but many of these happy customers will become an activated salesforce and invite others. How do you do it? Simple: Email or text your list offering a bonus if people tell their friends. For example, you might offer "one month free" or "a special discount code" that could be used when folks email the specific link you've offered to a friend or family member.

The key here is to make the technology easy to use. Give them their own link. Or, if your product is a high-ticket item, you might even skin a landing page for your customer to use. The easiest way, though, is to offer a "friends and family" discount in the form of a specific coupon code they can pass along to others.

Give Your Customers a Helpful Tool They Can Use to Spread the Word

A few years ago, I utilized the services of a consulting firm that, as part of their system, asked me for a list of referrals. The request made me immediately uncomfortable. I felt like they wanted to use me for my friends, or worse, turn me into one of their salespeople.

That said, the service they provided was good, and had

they framed the request another way, I might have complied. Specifically, it would have been nice if they'd have created a small, educational video that would have been valuable to my friends. I'd much more quickly pass along a video than I would hand over my friends' email addresses.

Consider creating a PDF or video that you automatically send to new and happy clients along with an email that goes something like this:

> Dear Friend,
>
> Thanks for doing business with us. A number of our clients have wanted to tell their friends about how we help customers, but they aren't sure how to do so. We've put together a little video that will help your friends solve *X problem*. If you have any friends with *X problem*, feel free to send it along. We'd be happy to follow up with any of them, and we'll be sure to let you know whether we were able to help them, giving you all the credit!
>
> We know you value your relationships and so do we. If your friends are experiencing a problem we've helped you solve, we'd love to help them too. If there's anything else we can do, please let us know.
>
> Sincerely,
> Nancy
>
> PS. *X problem* can be frustrating. If you'd rather introduce us to your friend in person, just let us know. We are more than happy to meet with them in their place of business or at our office.

Offer a Reward

If you really want to prime the pump, offer a reward to existing clients who refer their friends. As I mentioned earlier, my wife has invited dozens of friends to try out Blue Apron, a company that sends ready-to-cook meals right to people's doors. Plenty of Betsy's friends have enjoyed the service and signed on for themselves. Betsy receives a reward from Blue Apron every time somebody signs up.

Another way to offer a reward is to start an affiliate program. You can offer your customers a 10 percent commission on the orders they bring to you. This system has generated millions of dollars for thousands of companies. A good affiliate program can do the work of an expensive salesforce if you structure the percentages well.

AUTOMATE THE WORK

The easiest, fastest referral system can be automated using Keap or any other CRM. Simply include any customer who places one or two orders in an automated campaign that offers them an educational video or PDF they can pass on, an added reward for telling their friends about you, or even a commission.

Some Real-World Referral Systems

Implementing a referral system takes work, but it's effective. Take some inspiration from these samples:

A 100 Percent Refund for Three New Referrals Within a Semester. This was the brainchild of an after-school test-prep academy that prepared high school students for the SAT and ACT college admissions test, but it could just as well have been an eye doctor or a massage therapist. Parents were given a referral card to hand out to friends, many of whom had kids around the same age. Each time one of the cards came back, the referrer was credited hundreds of dollars because these courses were expensive! When they referred three new registrants, the referrer was given a 100 percent refund. Sure, the kids were competing with test scores, but the parents ended up competing for referrals, and business skyrocketed. The business also offered special seminars for parents and students of the 100 Percent Referral Club.

Invite-a-Friend Coupons. When students signed up for golf lessons, the range offered each new student several coupons for a free bucket of golf balls for a friend. While it's an individual game, golf is a social sport since people enjoy playing together. The course experienced a 40 percent increase in students signing up for lessons because word of mouth spread so effectively.

Open-House Party. Whenever a home contractor finished a large-scale decking or remodel project, he asked the homeowners if they would be willing to throw an open-house party in exchange for a slight discount. Friends, family, and neighbors were invited to a cookout on the newly built deck. The contractor used this opportunity to explain how the work was done and pass out cards. With only a few open-house parties, the contractor filled his schedule for the following twelve months.

Free Follow-Up Photos. A wedding photographer in Syracuse, New York, offered couples a free follow-up portrait on their one-year anniversary if the couple provided three referrals at the time of the wedding. She also followed up with cards to the entire bridal party, expressing how much of a pleasure it was to photograph them. Needless to say, business boomed because people who are in wedding parties often end up getting married soon themselves, especially if they catch the bouquet!

WHAT'S YOUR MARKETING PLAN?

In my twenties I spent an entire year playing chess. Nearly every day I met a friend at a coffee shop and we'd go at it for a couple of hours. My skills improved, and I ended up winning more than half my matches until another friend started showing up. He beat me every time, usually within twenty moves.

The reason? I knew a lot about the philosophy of chess, but I didn't have what's referred to as an *opening*. Before sitting down to play, my more skilled opponent already knew his first five moves. This opening strategy was critical to his success. Once I memorized a few openings of my own, I started to win again.

If the StoryBrand BrandScript is a foundation, the seven marketing pieces (or strategies) that make up the StoryBrand Messaging and Marketing Campaign should serve as your opening moves. These seven simple yet powerful tools have been used by countless businesses to increase their revenue.

Consider the messaging and marketing campaign a checklist. After you've created your StoryBrand BrandScript, get to work on each aspect of this playbook and watch as your customers engage and your company grows. If you want help creating your StoryBrand Messaging and Marketing Campaign or if you want a marketing coach to help you create several of them, perhaps one for each division or product you sell, you can find a directory of the marketing coaches I have personally certified at MarketingMadeSimple.com.

If you're serious about creating a StoryBrand Messaging and Marketing Campaign, spend an hour at StoryBrand.AI and have the StoryBrand Brain create your campaign. When you do, you will get a robust report including a tagline, one-liner, wireframed website, lead generator, follow-up emails, sales script, narrative scripts for YouTube videos and social media, podcast prompts and topics, bonus ideas to create urgency, upsell product ideas, plug-and-play social media posts plus industry trends specific to your industry.

AFTERWORD

I've lost count of how many StoryBrand clients we've helped in the last decade, but it's certainly tens of thousands. My hope is that this book has been the best marketing investment you've ever made because it's helped you improve your existing marketing so much and also because it has inspired you to create even more marketing and messaging that works.

You probably have a much more interesting product or service than you realize. You've likely just not found your audience yet. Do not be disheartened. When you clarify your message, your audience will find you.

If you really want to internalize the framework or introduce the framework to friends and coworkers, listen to and share *StoryBrand Radio Theater Presents: Pete and Joe Save Their Mother's Company* on Audible or Youtube.com/@storybrand. We had a lot of fun recording that story, and I even get to play a bit role as the ghost of myself. You will have to listen to find out what I'm talking about. By the way, that's called a cliff-hanger, and you should incorporate a few of those into your marketing too!

STORYBRAND.AI

At StoryBrand.AI, you can use the StoryBrand Brain to create a BrandScript to clarify your message for free. The StoryBrand Brain can also create a StoryBrand Messaging and Marketing Campaign that includes: a tagline, one-liner, wireframed website, lead generator, follow-up emails, sales script, narrative scripts for YouTube videos and social media, podcast prompts and topics, bonus ideas to create urgency, upsell product ideas, plug-and-play social media posts plus industry trends specific to your industry. Our messaging and marketing campaign is perfect for small business owners, anybody running a company, marketing and sales directors, and account representatives. The campaign generator will also work to brainstorm a new product or brand.

ACKNOWLEDGMENTS

I'm grateful to Kyle Reid, Tyler Ginn, Chad Cannon, Emily Pastina, Tim Schurrer, Koula Callahan, Kyle Reed, Avery Csorba, J. J. Peterson, Chad Snavely, Suzanne Norman, Matt Harris, Aaron Alfrey, Lucas Alley, Tyler Bridges, Sam Buchholz, Zach Grusznski, Dagne Saito, Andy Harrison, Hannah Hitchcox, Marlee Joseph, Kelley Kirker, Kari Loncar, Ben Landheer, Josh Landrum, Paige McQueen, Amanda Mitchell, James Mitchell, Carey Murdock, Luke Pastina, Etsy Pitman, Bobby Richards, Macy Robison, Prentice Sims, Hilary Smith, James Sweeting, Jordan Tatro, Taylor Wellman, and Betsy Miller for helping me build StoryBrand. Their tireless work on behalf of our clients has helped thousands of businesses connect with customers, hire more people, and solve their customers' problems. This team is more than a staff; they are family.

I'm also grateful to Mike Kim, who helped me edit the first edition of this book. Webster Younce, Heather Skelton, and Brigitta Nortker of HarperCollins also contributed significantly to the book with their careful edits and additions.

Special thanks to Brandon Dickerson for his help fleshing out commercial evidence for the framework.

Lastly, thank you. Thank you for daring to make and sell things, for solving customers' problems, helping heroes find homes, and putting your customers' stories above your own. As I said in the beginning, may you be richly rewarded for putting your customer first and inviting them into a story that solves their problem and helps them win.

ABOUT THE AUTHOR

Donald Miller is the CEO of Coach Builder and StoryBrand.AI. He is the author of several books including *Building a StoryBrand*, *Hero on a Mission*, and *How to Grow Your Small Business*. His latest book is *Coach Builder: How to Turn Your Expertise into a Profitable Coaching Career*. Donald lives in Nashville, Tennessee with his wife, Elizabeth and their daughter, Emmeline.

PRAISE FOR THE STORYBRAND FRAMEWORK

"Before StoryBrand, customers weren't seeing themselves in our offering. We're a staffing agency that specializes in helping companies find and hire the right people. We help companies post job applications, we test candidates, and we provide software for applicant tracking. Sadly, our message, though, was all about us. We were talking about our strengths rather than the customer's needs. Also, our marketing material was too complex and hard to understand. After bringing in a StoryBrand facilitator, we clarified our message and made it about our customer. We revised our sales process and started listening to our customers' needs, asking them about their external problems and how those problems were making them feel in their daily work. The results were immediate. We created our BrandScript in December and spent the next couple of months executing our new messaging across every part of the customer journey. Within seven months we'd seen a 118 percent increase in overall revenue. Yes, that means we more than doubled sales. We also saw a 276 percent increase in the number of paying customers during that same time period. And we're still growing. In the last six months, we've been increasing revenue 9 percent month over month, which really adds up!"

—Edwin Jansen, head of marketing, Fitzii

"Lipscomb University is one of the fastest-growing universities in the Southeast, so it was no small task to get all the stories of our school clear and on mission. We knew it was important, and so we brought in StoryBrand to deliver a workshop to our entire faculty. Without question, it helped us understand who we were, who we were serving, and what we needed to communicate to offer value. After StoryBrand, each department felt like they were a subplot in the greater story of Lipscomb. The most tangible way we saw results was through our outreach to the community. We stopped positioning ourselves as the hero and instead began to serve the greater collective vision of Nashville. All of this culminated in a series called Imagine, in which we brought in the mayor of Nashville, Governor Bill Haslam, and former president George W. Bush to speak about how Nashville and Lipscomb could positively contribute to the world. We stopped talking about us and we started serving as a guide to the community around us. Since this dramatic pivot, the renewed energy around a greater vision in which Lipscomb would play a part has resulted in more than $50 million in donations that will go toward development. I'd say the results have been fantastic."

—John Lowry, vice president of development, Lipscomb University

"I was asked to give a TED Talk about the work I do advocating for proton therapy as a treatment for cancer. As I reviewed the enormous binder of material I wanted to cover, I realized the task was epic. There was no way I could boil down all I wanted to say into an eighteen-minute talk. After spending a single day with a StoryBrand facilitator, I had hope. We mapped out my talk on a whiteboard, and I agreed to leave most of the things I wanted to talk about on the editing room floor. The talk was easy to memorize, flowed like a short story, and engaged the audience from beginning to end. StoryBrand didn't just help me prepare my TED Talk, they helped me understand how to better approach the advocacy I'd been doing. It all comes down to simple, repeatable messages that grab the audience. Without StoryBrand, I'd have never been able to clarify my message and inform the audience about a cause I care so deeply about. With the help of StoryBrand, I hit a home run, or more appropriately, I landed a triple luxe."

—Scott Hamilton, Olympic gold medalist, founder of Scott Cares, and three-time cancer survivor

"These Numbers Have Faces is a nonprofit working to provide educational equality in sub-Saharan Africa, where only five percent of the population will attend university. Before StoryBrand, our biggest problem was we were playing the hero. We talked more about our nonprofit than we did about our students or our donors. When we did talk about our students' problems, we talked about their external problems rather than their internal problems, which we now know is a limited way of approaching our messaging. After attending the StoryBrand workshop, we overhauled our messaging. In our emails, we began to connect donors with the narrative of the mission, and on social media, we told the stories of our heroic students. We used our StoryBrand BrandScript to draft our end-of-year report that got significant attention. As of today, we are on track to raise more money this year than ever before. We blew our fundraising goal out of the water. We will go into next year with the largest cash advantage we've ever had. Team, donor, and student morale is at an all-time high."

—Justin Zoradi, executive director of These Numbers Have Faces

"When EntreLeadership grew from a brand that basically just offered live events into a full-fledged coaching service for small business owners, we started experiencing challenges in how to explain what we did and how we did it. Even though we'd been writing copy and updating our website for years, the reality was that most of the time we were just guessing at the best way to say things. As a result, people didn't understand our coaching service the way we thought they did. This was frustrating because the value of our program was so obvious to us. The mistake we made was assuming it was obvious to our customers too. We were clear . . . they were confused. That doesn't sell. I knew we were capable of more conversions and more effective connection with our audience, but I wasn't sure how to get there. It wasn't until we brought in a StoryBrand facilitator and sat down as a team to overhaul our entire world through the lens of the StoryBrand framework that we became crystal clear on how to explain our coaching service. EntreLeadership has grown significantly, and we are tracking to more than double membership in the next two years. The StoryBrand framework is an invaluable resource, and I now expect our marketers to use it in everything we create."

—Daniel Tardy, vice president of EntreLeadership, Ramsey Solutions

"At Marie Mae we sell beautiful paper products and office supplies. Before StoryBrand, our marketing efforts were a jumbled mess. I once overheard a close friend talking about Marie Mae Company . . . and it was nothing close to what we were doing. I attended a StoryBrand Marketing Workshop and learned we were talking about the wrong things in our marketing copy. This was life changing for our start-up. We used the framework to simplify our message down to a single tagline. We started focusing more on the meaningful work our customers were doing and showing how they could make an even bigger impact around the world just by choosing office products that also make an impact. We simplified our website using the SB7 framework, and all of our marketing emails are now run through the SB7 filter as well. In the year since we implemented the StoryBrand framework, we have increased our revenue by 20x and gotten our products into the hands of 250,000 people. We attribute this success largely to the clarity in our story and the shift in our marketing messages. We are grateful."

—Jillian Ryan, founder of Marie Mae Company

"Before StoryBrand, I felt like my marketing was falling flat. I felt like my business had hit a ceiling. Going through the framework taught me I was talking about my programs all wrong. I used the StoryBrand framework to recreate my sales material from scratch. It took quite a bit of effort to rethink the whole thing. I dipped my toes in the water by making a few changes to key pieces of marketing material, being sure they spoke directly to my clients' needs. I relaunched my program with my new sales materials and saw a massive response. A campaign that would have typically brought in $6,000 to $9,000 brought in more than $40,000. StoryBrand is the most practical, applicable, implementable, logical, simple, useful marketing program I've ever experienced. It's going to change everything in my business, and I'm just getting started."

—Jenny Shih, business coach

"We often got a great deal of confusion when we tried to answer the question, 'So what do you *do*?' We were regularly frustrated by the fact that we had a huge body of organizational knowledge about our own work, and it required at least an hour to convey it to people. As a start-up, nonprofit organization, our revenue (donations) were barely enough to keep us afloat. We knew a big reason for this was that our model was a bit complex and it didn't get communicated with clarity, leaving potential donors confused. We took a big risk and chose to send our entire US team (three people) to StoryBrand—a risk that ate up a significant cut of our cash on hand. StoryBrand was indispensable for us. In the days following StoryBrand, we made a hard pivot on our communications strategy. Over the course of a couple of months, we went from an organization on the verge of collapse to an organization that was thriving. In Q4 alone (post-StoryBrand), we literally tripled our annual revenue. Now Mavuno has expanded its reach by 400 percent in eastern Congo, and we are ending extreme poverty for thousands of Congolese. We are making dramatic change for some of the most vulnerable people in one of the world's most war-torn environments. We are postured for enormous scale, and that is due in large part to StoryBrand. Thank you for helping us change the world."

—Daniel Myatt, CEO of Mavuno

STORYBRAND RESOURCES

WANT TO HELP OTHER BUSINESSES WITH THEIR MESSAGING AND MARKETING STRATEGY?

BECOME A STORYBRAND CERTIFIED COACH

It's like being part of the best marketing agency in the world—except you maintain 100% control and ownership of your business. Whether you're a copywriter, social media marketer, graphic designer, web designer, web developer, marketing consultant, or agency owner, the StoryBrand coach program will give you proven frameworks to help you deliver exceptional results for clients and grow your business. Apply to become a StoryBrand certified coach now at StoryBrand.com/Coach.

WANT TO LEARN VIA AN ONLINE COURSE?

Get the StoryBrand Course on Business Made Simple

Want to dive deeper into the StoryBrand framework and go through a course to create your BrandScript? The StoryBrand Online Course will help you create your BrandScript while providing numerous examples and expert tips along the way. Once you're done with the course, you will have a compelling message you can use to create websites, keynotes, elevator pitches, and much more. Get access to the StoryBrand Online Course in the Business Made Simple Platform at BusinessMadeSimple.com/StoryBrand.

WANT YOUR TEAM TO UNDERSTAND AND IMPLEMENT THE STORYBRAND FRAMEWORK?

Book a StoryBrand Private Workshop

If you want to align your team, grow your business, and optimize your marketing strategy, the StoryBrand Private Workshop will help you do that. You'll spend 1.5 days with one of our expert facilitators who will help you clarify your message, unify your team, and develop a marketing strategy that works. Our facilitators will even take a look at your existing marketing materials once your BrandScript is created. Book a workshop now at StoryBrand.com/PrivateWorkshops.

WANT YOUR SALES TEAM TO CLOSE MORE SALES?

Book a StoryBrand Sales Transformation Training

If you want your sales team to learn how to use the power of storytelling to close more sales, book a StoryBrand Sales Transformation Training. Your sales team will learn how to invite customers into a story and position your products as the solution your customers have been looking for. Your sales team will walk away with 7 key talking points to use in every sales conversation so they can close more deals and drive revenue for your business. Book a StoryBrand Sales Transformation Training now at StoryBrandSales.com.

CREATE A STORYBRAND MESSAGING AND MARKETING CAMPAIGN

GET YOUR CUSTOM TAGLINE, WIREFRAMED WEBSITE, AND MORE

When you go to StoryBrand.AI, you can use our artificial intelligence tool to generate your BrandScript, tagline, one-liner, wireframed website, lead generator, follow-up emails, sales script, narrative scripts for YouTube videos and social media, podcast prompts and topics, bonus ideas to create urgency, upsell product ideas, plug-and-play social media posts plus industry trends specific to your industry. The StoryBrand Messaging and Marketing report is your secret weapon to grow your business.

NOTES

Chapter 2: The Secret Weapon That Will Grow Your Business

1. Samantha Sharf, "The World's Largest Tech Companies 2016: Apple Bests Samsung, Microsoft and Alphabet," *Forbes*, May 26, 2016, http://www.forbes.com/sites/samanthasharf/2016/05/26/the-worlds-largest-tech-companies-2016-apple-bests-samsung-microsoft-and-alphabet/#2b0c584d89ee.
2. "Alfred Hitchcock: Quotes," IMDB, accessed July 29, 2024, http://m.imdb.com/name/nm0000033/quotes.

Chapter 3: The Simple SB7 Framework

1. "Great Presentations: Understand the Audience's Power," *Duarte*, http://www.duarte.com/great-presentations-understand-the-audiences-power/.
2. Ronald Reagan, "Farewell Address to the Nation," January 11, 1989, The American Presidency Project, http://www.presidency.ucsb.edu/ws/index.php?pid=29650.

3. "President Bill Clinton—Acceptance Speech," *PBS Newshour*, August 29, 1996, http://www.pbs.org/newshour/bb/politics-july-dec96-clinton_08-29/.
4. Claire Suddath, "A Brief History of Campaign Songs: Franklin D. Roosevelt," *Time*, accessed July 29, 2024, http://content.time.com/time/specials/packages/article/0,28804,1840981_1840998_1840901,00.html.

Chapter 4: A Character

1. Viktor E. Frankl, *Man's Search for Meaning* (Boston: Beacon Press, 2006).

Chapter 5: Has a Problem

1. James Scott Bell, *Plot & Structure: Techniques and Exercises for Crafting a Plot That Grips Readers from Start to Finish* (Cincinnati, OH: Writer's Digest Books, 2004), 12.
2. "Why CarMax?," CarMax.com, accessed February 10, 2017, https://www.carmax.com/car-buying-process/why-carmax.
3. "The Just 100: America's Best Corporate Citizens," *Forbes*, May 2016, http://www.forbes.com/companies/carmax/.

Chapter 6: And Meets a Guide

1. Bell, *Plot & Structure*, 31–32.
2. Christopher Booker, *The Seven Basic Plots: Why We Tell Stories* (London: Continuum, 2004), 194.
3. Ben Sisario, "Jay Z Reveals Plans for Tidal, a Streaming Music Service," *New York Times*, March 30, 2015, https://www.nytimes.com/2015/03/31/business/media/jay-z-reveals-plans-for-tidal-a-streaming-music-service.html.
4. Sisario, "Jay Z Reveals Plans for Tidal."
5. "Clinton vs. Bush in 1992 Debate," YouTube video, 4:08, posted by "Seth Masket," March 19, 2007, https://www.youtube.com/watch?v=7ffbFvKlWqE.

6. Infusionsoft home page, accessed February 9, 2017, https://www.infusionsoft.com.
7. Amy Cuddy, *Presence: Bringing Your Boldest Self to Your Biggest Challenges* (New York: Little, Brown, 2015), 71–72.

Chapter 7: Who Gives Them a Plan

1. "Why CarMax?," CarMax.com, accessed February 10, 2017, https://www.carmax.com/car-buying-process/why-carmax.
2. Arlena Sawyers, "Hot Topics, Trends to Watch in 2016," *Automotive News*, December 28, 2015, http://www.autonews.com/article/20151228/RETAIL04/312289987/hot-topics-trends-to-watch-in-2016.

Chapter 9: That Helps Them Avoid Failure

1. Susanna Kim, "Allstate's 'Mayhem' Is Biggest Winner of College Bowl," ABC News, January 2, 2015, http://abcnews.go.com/Business/allstates-mayhem-biggest-winner-college-bowl/story?id=27960362.
2. Daniel Kahneman and Amos Tversky, "Prospect Theory: An Analysis of Decision Under Risk," *Econometrica* 47, no. 2 (March 1979): 263–91, https://www.jstor.org/stable/1914185.
3. Dominic Infante, Andrew Rancer, and Deanna Womack, *Building Communication Theory* (Long Grove, IL: Waveland Press, 2003), 149.
4. Infante, Rancer, and Womack, *Building Communication Theory*, 150.

Chapter 10: And Ends in a Success

1. Stewart D. Friedman, "The Most Compelling Leadership Vision," *Harvard Business Review*, May 8, 2009, https://hbr.org/2009/05/the-most-compelling-leadership.

Chapter 11: People Want Your Brand to Participate in Their Transformation

1. "Hello Trouble," Vimeo video, 1:44, posted by Adam Long, February 13, 2013, https://vimeo.com/59589229.